T2-CSE-516

Working Together

DATE DUE

Working Together:
Fundamentals of Group Decision Making

RUDOLPH F. VERDERBER

University of Cincinnati

Wadsworth Publishing Company
Belmont, California

A division of Wadsworth, Inc.

Senior Editor: Rebecca Hayden
Production: Del Mar Associates
Designer: John Odam
Copy Editor: Andrea Matyas

Printed in the United States of America

1 2 3 4 5 6 7 8 9 10—86 85 84 83 82

Library of Congress Cataloging in Publication Data

Verderber, Rudolph F.
    Working together.

    Includes index.
    1. Decision-making, Group.   I. Title.
HM131.V438   302.3   81-19778
ISBN 0-534-01100-4 (pbk.)   AACR2

Photo credits
2: ©Ed Buryn Jeroboam, Inc.
42: ©Suzanne Arms/Jeroboam, Inc.
136: ©Emilio Mercado/Jeroboam, Inc.
166: ©Don Ivers/Jeroboam, Inc.

PREFACE

Working Together is an introduction to group decision-making skills. To produce this work, I have combined what I believe are the results of some of the best group research with conclusions I have reached through my years of teaching experience. The combination of reading about skills and practicing them in your decision-making groups should enable you to become an effective group communicator.

Getting the most from either this book or from your practice will require your cooperation. Too many people see group work as a painless way of getting a job done. They assume that somehow the group will generate and process information with no special time or effort required from the individual. But such an approach to group decision making will not work; regardless of the qualifications of the participants, each person will have to work hard to ensure the best possible decision.

You may, of course, wonder whether your participation can really influence group outcome. Although one person's skill cannot guarantee group success, even one well-prepared, skilled individual can make a difference. In a group where two or more are knowledgeable, skilled, and willing to work, the potential exists for arriving at the best possible decision.

This book has four parts. Part One, "Introduction to Group Decision Making," is a three-chapter unit. The first chapter defines group decision making and discusses the ramifications of each aspect of the definition. Chapter 2 establishes criteria for determining when groups should make decisions. Chapter 3 considers seven criteria that are likely to be met by effective groups.

Part Two, "The Group Decision-Making Process," outlines the steps of the process: determining the group's goal, analyzing the problem, researching, communicating, using supplementary approaches, coping with conflict, and drawing conclusions. Some steps can be individually accomplished by members of the group prior to the group meeting, some can be started by an individual and finished in the group, and some can only be accomplished through group interaction.

Part Three, "Leading Groups," considers both the theory of leadership and the responsibilities a leader has in the group process. Since these two chapters are presented as a self-contained unit, instructors can assign them at the most appropriate time.

Part Four, "Analyzing Group Effectiveness," is a one-chapter unit that provides a rationale for evaluating group decision making. Since evaluation will take place throughout the term, instructors may wish to integrate the study of this chapter with the study of the decision-making process.

I wish to thank the following reviewers for their thoughtful and critical comments on the manuscript. Their suggestions helped me in making many decisions in the final stages of revision.

Mary F. Beasley, Louisiana Tech University
Stephen Green, University of Cincinnati
George D. Losee, Humboldt State University
James P. McGlone, Seton Hall University
James Mancuso, Mesa Community College
Dorotha O. Norton, University of Tennessee, Martin
Suzanne J. Vadasz, McHenry County College

CONTENTS

Working Together

ONE

INTRODUCTION TO GROUP DECISION MAKING

Many important business, industrial, and governmental decisions are made in groups. In this three-chapter introductory unit, we define group decision making, determine when groups are most appropriate for decision making, and establish criteria for group effectiveness.

1

DEFINING GROUP DECISION MAKING

It is likely that in your lifetime, regardless of your occupation, you will spend more than 9,000 hours—roughly one year—in meetings![1] Moreover, the greater your responsibility within a given organization, the *more* time you will spend in meetings. In a recent study of business practice, for instance, it was found that nearly 40 percent of business management time is spent in group and consultation contexts.[2] Even in college teaching, a profession that is regarded for highly individual work, a great deal of time is spent in group work. The average faculty member simultaneously serves on one college committee, two or three departmental committees, one university standing committee, and two or three subcommittees—for a total of about 11 hours per week.[3]

Despite the extensive time involved, many people perceive their group work as a waste of time. Listen to the tone of voice of a person who says, "Well, I'm off to a meeting," and you will sense the frustration of someone who would rather do anything than attend a meeting.

The goal of this book is to provide you with a procedure for making your group decision making more productive. By using a more effective method, your group can save time. And when you consider the dollar-per-hour cost of paying members of a group, you can see how saving time also saves an organization a great deal of money. Moreover, more effective methods improve morale—because ambiguity is lessened through clearer group goals and procedures. Finally, and perhaps most important, effective methods produce better decisions.

The opening unit of this book lays the groundwork for learning the skills that are the focus of the second unit. In Chapter 2, we will lay down the criteria for determining when a group is the best agent for decision making. In Chapter 3, we will examine the profile of an effective group. Here we will

---

[1]Michael Doyle and David Straus, *How to Make Meetings Work* (New York: Wyden Books, 1976), p. 4.

[2]Research by Philip Marvin, professor of professional development, University of Cincinnati, reported by Jeanne Jahnigen, "How Do Executives Pass Their Time?" *UC This Week* (January 16, 1981), p. 2.

[3]Gerald M. Goldhaber, *Organizational Communication* (Dubuque, Iowa: Wm. C. Brown, 1974), p. 214.

concentrate on defining group decision making and exploring the various aspects of that definition.

Group decision making is two or more people communicating with one another using logical means, in public or in private, to arrive at mutually satisfying decisions. Although there is some controversy about the smallest number that constitutes a group, we will restrict the size to two or more. In Chapter 3, we will analyze the variable of size in some detail. For now, let us turn to the other aspects of the definition: communication, reliance on logical means, and public and private contexts.

Group Decision Making Involves Communication

It seems evident that two or more people can make mutually satisfying decisions only by communicating. Communication is a process that involves stimulating meaning in the mind of another person. If you communicate well, the meaning that the other person has is the same as or analogous to the meaning you intend. Thus, effective communication is the process of *sharing* meaning. Effective group communication involves the *people* doing the communicating sharing *messages* through oral *channels* with a minimum of *noise*.

People

The people who are communicating in groups fulfill the roles of sender and receiver—sometimes simultaneously. As senders, they form messages, which they attempt to communicate to others. As receivers, they process the messages sent to them and react both verbally and nonverbally.

The people in your decision-making group are products of their individual experiences, feelings, ideas, moods, occupations, religions, and so forth. As a result, the *meaning* sent by one person and the meaning received by the group may not be identical. For instance, when Art speaks of the importance of developing good jobs for students who are entering a co-op program, Art may mean jobs that are highly paid. To Glen, and perhaps to other members of the committee, a good job may be one that is stimulating, regardless of pay. Successful group communicators must take advantage of every available skill to present and to interpret meanings as clearly as possible so that the meanings are *shared*.

Messages

Messages are the content of group discussion. Meaning, symbols used, and form or organization are three of the key elements of messages.

Meanings are ideas and feelings. For example, you have ideas about how a group should prepare for its task, whether Tom's ideas are supportable, and the way Suzie is able to control the group. With each of these ideas you have accompanying feelings: you may feel good about the depth of preparation your group has shown, you may be embarrassed by Tom's lack of support for his statements, and you may be envious of Suzie's apparent ease in controlling the group. Meanings cannot be directly moved from one person's mind to the mind of another. We need a vehicle to communicate our meanings and to create similar meanings in someone else's mind.

To express our ideas and feelings to others, we use the vehicle of symbols. Symbols are words or actions that represent meaning. Symbols can be communicated with the voice and with the body. As we speak, our mind chooses words to convey messages. At the same time, however, our facial expressions, gestures, and tone of voice—all nonverbal cues—affect the meaning of the message. When we listen to others, we receive the verbal and nonverbal cues and assign meanings to them. The process of transforming ideas and feelings into symbols is called *encoding*. The process of transforming the symbols we receive into ideas and feelings is called *decoding*.

The communication process probably has become so automatic for you that you rarely think consciously about encoding or decoding. When you listen to a tentative plan for resolving some of the problems that commuters face on your campus, and you think the plan is good, you might say something like, "That sounds like a great plan—I think it will work." You are not likely to think, "I wonder what symbols will best express the thought I am now having." Occasionally, however, as when you grope for words, especially when you feel the right word is on the tip of your tongue, you may become aware of the process.

Symbols that carry meanings are not always used intentionally. Most of your verbal communication is done with a purpose. Yet, while you are talking, you may be sending complementary or conflicting messages through unintentional nonverbal cues. For example, Martha turns to Paul and says, "You can get a summary of what we discussed today typed up by noon tomorrow, can't you?" and Paul replies, "Sure, no problem." Yet, Martha may note a tone of uneasiness in Paul's voice. Although Paul intends to convey a note of confidence with the words "Sure, no problem," the nonverbal cues he is sending through his tone of voice may unintentionally betray his verbal message. Had his tone been perceived as confident, the nonverbal cues would have reinforced the verbal meaning. Instead, the unintentional message contradicted the intentional one. Both the intentional and the unintentional use of symbols are important to the sharing of meaning.

The third element of message is form. When an idea or feeling has many parts, the sender may need to communicate it in sections or in a certain order so that the receiver will not be confused. Although message form is especially important in public speaking, when one person is talking for a relatively long time, it is still important in a group setting. For instance, Julia tells the group about her plan for helping commuters develop a sense of identification with the campus. If her explanation moves logically from point to point, the group is far more likely to follow her than if she provides bits and pieces in random order.

In Chapter 7, "Discussing the Question," we will consider the skills that group members need to learn and to practice to improve sending and receiving messages.

Channels

The *channel* is both the route traveled by the message and the means of transportation. Spoken words are carried from one person to another by air waves. Facial expressions, gestures, and movements are carried by light waves. Usually, the more channels used to carry a message, the more the communication will succeed. Although most group communication is two channelled (light and sound), participants can and do communicate messages by smell and touch. A fragrant scent and a firm handshake may be as important in communicating a person's meanings as the words and gestures.

Noise

A person's ability to interpret, understand, and respond to symbols is often hampered by noise. *Noise* is any stimulus that gets in the way of sharing meaning. Your success as a group communicator may often depend on how you cope with external, internal, and semantic noises.

External noises are the sights, sounds, and other stimuli that draw attention away from the message. For instance, if during a meeting about a campus problem your attention is drawn to the sound of a power lawnmower outside the window, you may be unable to concentrate on the discussion. External noise does not have to be a sound to be distracting—it may also be a sight. Perhaps during the same discussion an extremely attractive man or woman looks at you with what you perceive as a particularly engaging expression. For that moment at least, your attention is likely to be drawn toward that person.

Internal noises are the thoughts and feelings that intrude on your mind while you are attempting to pay attention to someone or something else. Perhaps while a speaker uses an example of food distribution to make a point, the thought of food causes you to daydream about dinner. If you have tuned out the speaker and tuned in a daydream, a past conversation, or an irrelevant feeling, you have created internal noise.

The third type of noise, and perhaps the most difficult to cope with, is semantic. *Semantic noises* are the differences in meanings that people get from the same words. Because your perceptions and experiences differ from those of other people in your group, you may have different ideas and feelings about even relatively simple words. Suppose a fellow student tells you that her professor will be reading a paper at a forthcoming convention. If you think that "reading a paper" means what people do to find out the day's news rather than giving an oral report on research, you may not understand her message. Since meaning depends on your own experience, you may at times decode a word or phrase to mean something different from the sender's intended meaning. When this happens, you have semantic noise.

Group Decision Making Relies on Logical Means

Whereas individual decisions can be based on emotion or trust, or made without any basis at all, group decision making relies on the logical means of analysis, evidence, and reasoning. In short, good decision making is based on information.

A group member begins with the premise that a decision cannot be made unless the group has the necessary facts and opinions. Occasionally, a group will have an outside agency provide the needed information to make a decision, or a group may have the expertise to make a decision. More often than not, however, a group's effectiveness will depend on the information-gathering capabilities of its members. Effective group members are good researchers. In Chapter 6, "Researching the Question," we will consider how to get necessary information.

A logical approach to decision making extends beyond looking for and finding material; it also requires careful analysis and reasoning. Analysis determines the subquestions that must be answered to provide a logical basis for the decision. Reasoning draws logical conclusions from the information the group has presented. In Chapter 5, we will consider procedures for analyzing questions; in Chapter 9, we will discuss reasoning.

A group achieves its goals through discussion of information. *Discussion* is informal interaction in which all participate freely and equally; it is marked by cooperation among participants, and it depends on objectivity in the presentation or materials.

In addition, discussion is a form of inquiry that requires participants to ask questions that probe the nature of the decision they hope to make. The answers to those questions lead the group to rational decisions. The goal of discussion is to arrive at conclusions that are a sum of the thinking of the entire group.

Although discussion is the ideal, decision making is likely to result from debate and persuasion as much as from discussion. *Debate* is an adversary approach to decision making involving the clash of opposing sides of a topic.

Debate is marked by an attitude of competition rather than cooperation among participants. Although debate procedure depends on objective analysis of materials, that analysis is presented from a position of advocacy. The discussant *inquires;* the debater *advocates.* Debaters present their side with solid reasons and evidence and look for and attack weaknesses in the opposition's argument. Debaters seek to win the audience, or more likely its noncommitted members, to their side by virtue of the power of their argument.

When the give-and-take objective approach of discussion breaks down, group members will often begin to debate various issues. Once a point is debated and resolved, group members should attempt to regain their objectivity and their inquiring approach to the material. Continuous debate on all aspects of a topic will tend to destroy the cohesiveness of a decision-making group. Thus, if you are always seen as a debater, you may be viewed as excessively argumentative and more interested in winning than in resolving the issues in a mutually agreeable way. At times debate cannot, and probably should not, be avoided. But total debate should be kept to a minimum.

Whereas debate occurs when discussion breaks down to diametrically opposed views, *persuasion* occurs when group members become so convinced of a position that they try to draw others to their point of view. Persuasion is a conscious, usually verbal attempt by one or more members of the group to influence other members. As with debate, persuasion is marked by the advocacy of a particular position. However, the persuader does not attempt to present both sides of the issue. The persuader says, "I see the benefits of a particular point of view." The persuader then supplies the reasons and the evidence in support of that view. But the persuader may still maintain enough objectivity to see the strength of an opposing point of view. Persuasion often occurs when the group is neutral about the issue or is mildly supportive of the persuader's position.

Decision-Making Contexts

Another major part of the definition of decision-making groups is context. Discussions may take place in public or in private. Public discussions are those that take place before or for the benefit of an audience. Private discussions are limited to those directly involved. Two common forms of public discussion are the symposium and the panel. Two common forms of private discussion are the action group and the committee.

Symposia and Panels

A *symposium* is a discussion in which a limited number of participants (usually three to five) present individual speeches of similar length that deal with the same subject. After the planned speeches, the participants in the symposium may discuss their reactions with each other and respond to questions from the listening audience. At the end, the participants may arrive at a mutually agreeable decision. Although a good symposium will provide information for decision making, the decision itself is usually in the hands of another body. Because a symposium does not use the skills we will be considering, we will not talk about it further in the book.

A *panel* discussion is one in which the participants, usually four to eight, discuss a topic spontaneously, under the direction of a leader, following a planned agenda. After the formal discussion, the audience is often encouraged to question the participants. A panel may often proceed in the manner suggested in later chapters of this book. Since the panel has an audience, however, time constraints usually keep it from accomplishing more than superficial coverage of the topic. Moreover, even when the panel has sufficient time to delve into the topic, the decisions it makes seldom carry much weight since the group is without the means for implementing its solution.

Action Groups and Committees

The group decision making you are more likely to be part of is private. Private discussions are likely to involve all those who are affected by a decision, or representatives of the larger group. Sometimes the decision-making group has the authority to implement the decision; sometimes the group is authorized only to report or recommend its decision to the larger group or to the larger group's presiding officer.

An *action group* is a group of people drawn together as the result of a common problem. For instance, neighbors might get together to oppose the building of a condominium in a neighborhood that had previously been zoned to prohibit such construction. All of this action group's efforts would be directed to approaches they can use to register their opposition. Often, action groups grow to such a size that they must call upon representatives to work in committees to discuss the issues. Sometimes the action group is small enough so that it can act as a decision-making body.

By far the most common experience you will have in group decision making will be in *committees*. There are basically two types of committees: standing committees and ad hoc committees.

A *standing committee* is one that is part of the structure of a larger group and is composed of a few of the members of that larger group. Most organizations have standing committees, such as social committees, budget committees, constitution committees, or ways and means committees. These small groups study the problems or topics that fall within their province and recommend courses of action to the larger group. Thus, if your organization is thinking of raising its fees, it might turn the issue over to the budget committee. If you do not have a standing committee to consider a given issue, your organization may decide to form an ad hoc committee.

Ad hoc committees are formed to study a particular issue. Organizations can form ad hoc committees, or a group of people may come together to form their own ad hoc committee. For instance, the department chairperson might appoint an ad hoc committee to study whether a new course should be offered, or a group of faculty members may, on their own, decide to form a group to consider this issue.

Ad hoc committees exist for set periods of time. An ad hoc committee is appointed or elected to deal with a particular problem or issue. An ad hoc committee usually meets until a decision is made, and then the group disbands. The skills we discuss in the remainder of this text will relate primarily to the work of private decision-making groups.

Summary

We have seen that a decision-making group comprises two or more people who communicate with one another using logical means, in public or in private, to arrive at mutually satisfying decisions.

From this definition we can see that group decision making involves communication. Communication stimulates meaning that is the same or analogous for all members of the group. Communication involves the people who are communicating, the contexts in which this communication takes place, the messages being communicated, and the channels through which the communication occurs.

Another aspect of group decision making is that it primarily uses logical means. Effective group decision making is an exercise in rational decision making. Ideally, most decision making will result from discussion, the informal interaction that follows a method of inquiry into the key questions that must be considered to arrive at a rational decision. But decision making may also be a result of debate, an adversary approach involving the clash of sides or of persuasion, the conscious attempt to influence other members of the group. All three methods depend on seeking reasons and evidence to justify a decision.

Although group decision making can take place in a symposium or a panel, it is more likely to occur in an action group or in a standing or ad hoc committee.

2

WHEN GROUPS DECIDE

Decisions, decisions—haven't we all experienced the frustration of trying to make the right decision? Like it or not, life requires one decision after another. Whether a decision is individual or organizational, whether it is relatively simple or important and complicated, the first question is, *who* will make the decision? Or to put the question in the context we are most concerned with, when should groups decide?

Although we know that some decisions are best made by groups and others are best made by individuals, most of us are inclined to select the decision-making agent intuitively, rather than through application of a set of criteria. Yet, who makes the decision is a vital but seldom-considered part of the decision-making process. Even though your goal is to become a more effective group decision maker, you will want to assure yourself that the decision you are helping to make is best handled by a group.

In this chapter we will explore the ways decisions can be made and will provide guidelines for choosing the most appropriate agency, whether person or group.

Decision-Making Models

The subject of models has a long history in decision-making science research. The recent work of Victor Vroom and his associates has provided a practical model that has gained considerable acceptance. In their analysis of leader behavior models, Vroom and Jago consider a taxonomy of decision processes. The following discussion is based on their analysis.[1] Basically, individuals have four choices for making a decision: they can delegate the decision-making power to someone else, they can make the decision themselves, they can consult with others and make the decision, or they can form a group and make the decision through group interaction. To explain and exemplify each choice, I created a hypothetical situation that has been true for many organizations during the last few years. Suppose Bill, the manager of the public relations division of an organization, is required to cut his unit's budget by

[1]Victor H. Vroom and Arthur G. Jago, "Decision Making as a Social Process: Normative and Descriptive Models of Leader Behavior," *Decision Sciences*, Vol. 5 (1974), p. 745.

10 percent. After assuring himself that cutting the budget is his only option, Bill proceeds to make his decision. Let us look at the various models of decision-making choices, and show how Bill would proceed using each.

Delegated Decision Making

A delegated decision model is one in which a person in authority gives (delegates) the decision-making power to another person or group of people. If Bill chooses to delegate the decision, he might give Paul, his assistant, the responsibility. Bill would tell Paul of the need for making a 10 percent budget cut and would assure Paul of complete authority to make the decision, which Bill will implement. Paul then has the option of making the decision himself or of making a consultive, a delegated, or a group decision.

Authoritarian Decision Making

An authoritarian decision is one made by the person in charge. If you choose to make an authoritarian decision, you can follow either of two models.

In the first authoritarian model, you make the decision yourself on the basis of information you have at your disposal. For example, Bill makes the decision on how to cut his division budget based on information that he has at his command as manager of the division.

In the second authoritarian model, you make the decision yourself on the basis of information at your disposal along with information that is provided by others. In getting information from others, you do not tell them why you want or need the information. Neither do you tell them what you will do with the information. Thus, Bill asks various employees in the division to provide data about expenditures. He then pools this information with his own data to arrive at a decision.

Consultive Decision Making

A consultive decision is one that is made after talking with one or more people about the problem. If you choose to make a consultive decision, you can follow one of two models.

First, you can share the problem with one or more persons individually. You would ask each person for ideas and information, but you would make the decision yourself. It is up to you to decide whether their input will have any influence on your decision. Using this model, Bill might consult Marge, who is close to the budgetary process; Paul, his assistant; and Mark, one of the division's most thoughtful members, for their opinions. After hearing what Marge, Paul, and Mark have to say, Bill would make the decision himself.

In the second consultive model, you would share the problem with a group of people at a meeting. You would solicit ideas and suggestions from the group, and you might even encourage each person to weigh and consider the various options. Again, it is up to you to decide whether the ideas, information, or suggestions of the group will influence your final decision. Using this model, Bill might ask Marge, Paul, and Mark to meet with him for an hour or so to talk about potential budget cuts. At the meeting, Bill would listen carefully to all ideas. Later, after reflecting on what was said and what he thought, Bill would make his decision.

Notice that although a consultive decision is participatory, the participation is at the information-presenting level, not at the decision-making level. The authority for the decision and the responsibility for its consequences rest with the person in charge.

Group Decision Making

Group decision making—the focus of this book—is done with full participation of all members. It may also follow two models.

In the first model, you share the problem with one other person. You both freely discuss the problem and arrive at a decision that is mutually agreeable. Bill meets with Paul, and they discuss ways of cutting the budget. At the end of the discussion, Bill and Paul arrive at a mutually agreeable decision.

In the second group decision-making model, you share the problem with a group of people. The group freely discusses the issue, following methods that we will consider later in this text, and arrives at a mutually agreeable decision. Bill calls a meeting with Marge, Paul, and Mark to discuss potential budget cuts. Bill participates in the discussion but does not try to influence the group. When the decision has been reached, Bill agrees to implement it.

We see then that a person basically has seven different models that grow from four categories of decision making. Four of the seven models involve some degree of participation. Yet, it is only the seventh, or last, model, group decision making, that is fully participatory.

Which model should Bill use? Which model would you use if you were responsible for cutting the budget? Which model would you use under other circumstances? For many, this decision is made intuitively. They select the model that "feels" right. Perhaps they will consider consequences. If they think they have sufficient power to make the decision, or if they think they can hold the support of those affected, they are likely to make the decision alone. At other times they may feel more comfortable seeking consultation or turning the decision over to another person or to a group.

For some people, the need for control is so great that any thought of bringing others into the decision-making process is rejected. Some leaders go through the motions of participatory decision making when in fact they hold complete control of the process. At the other end of the continuum are those who are so unsure of their decision-making capacity that they are always inclined to seek counsel or to turn the responsibility over to others. Although the intuitive method may lead to satisfactory results, determining the model of decision making solely by how people feel or how the plan fits their personalities will not lead to consistently good decision making.

Determining Appropriate Group Participation

During the last twenty years, a great deal of research has been done on decision-making methods. One of the major models now in use was developed by Victor Vroom and his associates.[2] From the Vroom model we can extract a series of general principles that indicate when group participation in the decision-making process is more or less desirable. After discussing these general recommendations, we will briefly examine the details of Vroom's decision-process flow chart.

Here are the basic guidelines for making a quick estimate of the appropriate degree of group participation in decision making:

1. Group participation may be more desirable when the quality of the decision is important. A better-documented and perhaps a higher-order decision will come from a group when quality is the most important variable. For instance, in our hypothetical example, budget cuts will affect the work of everyone in the public relations division. As a result, a high-quality decision is needed, and group participation would be most desirable.

Why does a group arrive at a higher-quality decision? Partly as a result of involving more people in the process. It is likely that a group of people will have more information and more collective knowledge than an individual leader or manager. This increase in information is especially likely when the source of information is individual experience or observation. Moreover, because there will be several people looking at the information, there is less likelihood that any important data that might affect the decision will be overlooked or that errors in judgment will occur. Good group analysis of information does not happen automatically. In later parts of this book we will consider procedures that will help you and your group analyze information and avoid errors in judgment.

2. Group participation may be more desirable when acceptance of a decision by other people or other groups is necessary to put the decision into practice. If Bill believes that a budget cut can be implemented only if key people in his division accept the fairness of the cut, Bill should use a group model for determining the nature of the budget cuts.

---

[2]V. H. Vroom and P. W. Yetton, *Leadership and Decision-Making* (Pittsburgh: University of Pittsburgh Press, 1973).

Although a leader or manager can demand that his or her decision be followed, in most cases implementation of such an edict must be carried out by individuals within the organization. Thus, involving members of the organization becomes a motivational factor. Because people who participate in decision making are more likely to become become ego involved in the implementation, they will work hard to see that the plan does not fail.

3.   Group participation may be more desirable when the participants are trusted to carefully consider the decision. Bill will be more inclined to involve a group if he believes the members will really commit themselves to the kind of preparation necessary for a high-quality decision. Since budget cuts will have important ramifications for key assistants in the division, a group decision seems warranted.

At least part of this trust is based on skills that group members have developed and on past experience with their involvement in decision making. If group members (or subordinates in an organizational context) are never called upon to participate, they never develop skills or a record of accomplishment. As a result, they are not likely to be trusted when important decisions are called for. Conversely, if group members are involved in at least some decision making and if they show care in their work, they are more likely to be trusted with important decisions.

4.   Group participation may be less desirable when a person has the necessary information to make a good decision. Bill will be less likely to use participatory means if he believes he has all the information he needs to make a judicious budget cut at his disposal. However, because budgetary considerations may be widespread throughout the division, the likelihood of his having this information is slight.

There may even be times when the leader or manager is the only person who has access to the necessary information. For example, in certain government, business, or industry situations, dissemination of information is restricted to those at higher levels. Under these circumstances, the individual must make the decision alone. But even in everyday situations there are many times when the leader has ready access to necessary information. Whether he or she then chooses to make the decision may involve some other factors we have considered.

5.   Group participation may be less desirable when a solution that has worked well in the past can be applied to this situation. If Bill has a model that he has recently used for a request to cut the budget, he will see less need to bring others into the decision-making process.

We make many decisions on the basis of precedent. If a situation seems to be much like another one in which a particular decision was successful, a similar decision might be adopted without the participation of group members.

6. Group participation may be desirable when time is limited and immediate action is necessary. Although it is unlikely that a request for a budget cut would be made at the last minute, it could happen. If the president of the organization has asked Bill to make a proposal immediately, Bill is more likely to make the decision himself.

The right timing may be vital to the success or failure of the venture, and the leader or manager may have to act quickly when the opportunity occurs. Because "time is short" may be a convenient excuse for usurpation of decision-making power, the leader or manager should be very careful before making the decision on that basis.

In these six guidelines Vroom and associates have specified the conditions under which various decision-making processes will result in an optimum decision. Because the Vroom model has been thoroughly tested, let us look at it in further detail.[3] As we have seen, the criteria that lie at the heart of their model are: (1) quality of a decision, (2) acceptance by others, and (3) time required. Now let us look at the model, Figure 2-1 on pages 20–21. Questions A–H represent the criteria for decisions—they should be answered yes or no. The decision-maker should work through the tree until an optimum decision process is indicated. At the bottom of the model are feasibility sets for group problems. The models that will work are listed from left to right, with the model requiring the fewest man-hours noted to the left. As you can see, the majority of decisions allow for group participation. In only a minority of instances is group participation inappropriate. But, other variables, of which time is perhaps the most important, will allow for other models to take precedence. Ivancevich and associates argue that "the Vroom-Yetton-Jago model represents an important improvement over classical decision theory with rather immediate implications for decision making as a social process."[4] To see for yourself how the decision tree works, state a few problems and work through the model with them.

Now that we have provided guidelines for determining when a group should make a decision, let us consider the final question of when you (as a manager or leader within an organizational structure) should participate in the group. Whether you delegate depends on whether there is a person you can

---

[3]V. H. Vroom and A. G. Jago, "On the Validity of the Vroom-Yetton model," *Journal of Applied Psychology,* Vol. 63 (1978), pp. 151–162.

[4]John M. Ivancevich, Andrew D. Szilagyi, Jr., and Marc J. Wallace, Jr., *Organizational Behavior and Performance* (Santa Monica, Calif.: Goodyear, 1977).

trust to provide strong leadership to the group. If so, you may want to let that person lead the group; if not, you may want to be a part of the group. A second important consideration is whether your presence will hinder the group process. If the perception of your status will overpower the group or in some way inhibit freedom of expression, then it is best that you avoid participation.

EXERCISES

1. Write down five important decisions you made or helped to make during the last month. Label the decision you made: (a) alone, with your own information; (b) alone, information from self and other sources; (c) consultative, advice from one other person; (d) consultative, advice from a group of people; (e) group, full participation, one other person; (f) group decision; or (g) delegated.

2. Was your choice for who made the decision a good one? By what criteria?

3. Take two of your important decisions and determine who should make them by working through the decision-making tree.

Summary

Although decisions can be made individually or in groups, the choice is not one that should be made on intuition alone.

Basically, decision making can follow four different methods: (1) delegated, in which a person in authority gives the decision-making power to another; (2) authoritarian, in which the person in charge makes the decision; (3) consultative, in which a person in charge makes a decision after talking with one or more individuals; and (4) group, in which one or more persons have full participation in the decision-making process.

Whether group participation is desirable can be decided on the basis of six guidelines. Participation is more desirable when: (1) the quality of the decision is important, (2) others must accept the decision before it can be implemented, and (3) participants are trusted to make careful decisions. Group participation is less desirable when: (1) a person has the necessary information to make a good decision, (2) a solution that has worked well in the past can be applied, and (3) time is limited.

A complete analysis of group versus individual decision-making is supplied in the Vroom decision-making tree.

A. Is there a quality requirement such that one solution is likely to be more rational than another?
B. Do I have sufficient info to make a high quality decision?
C. Is the problem structured?
D. Is acceptance of decision by subordinates critical to effective implementation?
E. If I were to make the decision by myself, is it reasonably certain that it would be accepted by my subordinates?

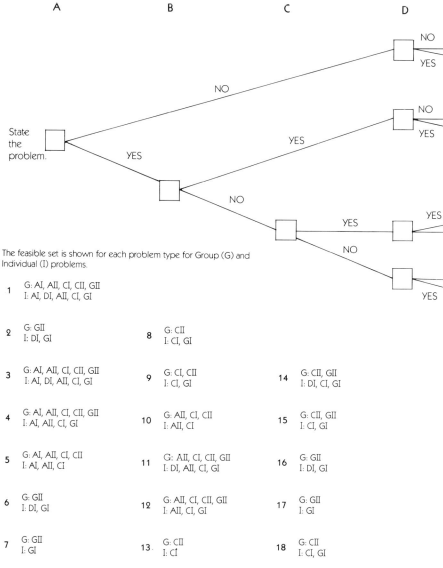

The feasible set is shown for each problem type for Group (G) and Individual (I) problems.

1   G: AI, AII, CI, CII, GII
    I: AI, DI, AII, CI, GI

2   G: GII
    I: DI, GI

8   G: CII
    I: CI, GI

3   G: AI, AII, CI, CII, GII
    I: AI, DI, AII, CI, GI

9   G: CI, CII
    I: CI, GI

14 G: CII, GII
    I: DI, CI, GI

4   G: AI, AII, CI, CII, GII
    I: AI, AII, CI, GI

10 G: AII, CI, CII
    I: AII, CI

15 G: CII, GII
    I: CI, GI

5   G: AI, AII, CI, CII
    I: AI, AII, CI

11 G: AII, CI, CII, GII
    I: DI, AII, CI, GI

16 G: GII
    I: DI, GI

6   G: GII
    I: DI, GI

12 G: AII, CI, CII, GII
    I: AII, CI, GI

17 G: GII
    I: GI

7   G: GII
    I: GI

13 G: CII
    I: CI

18 G: CII
    I: CI, GI

Figure 2-1. Decision-process flow chart for both individual and group problems.

F. Do subordinates share the organizational goals to be attained in solving this problem?
G. Is conflict among subordinates likely in preferred solutions? (This question is irrelevant to individual problems.)
H. Do subordinates have sufficient info to make a high quality decision?

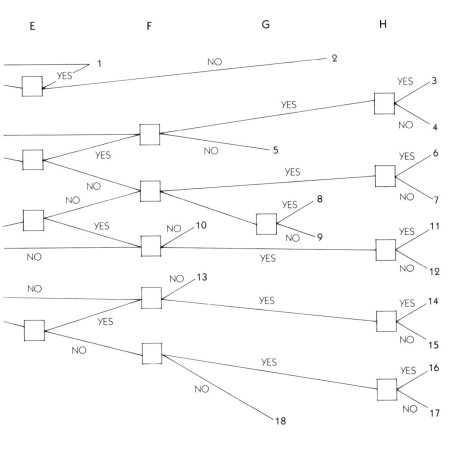

Reprinted from V. Vroom and A. Jago, "Decision Making as A Social Process: Normative and Descriptive Models of Leader Behavior," **Decision Sciences**, (1974), p. 748. By permission of American Institute for Decision Sciences.

3

PROFILE OF AN EFFECTIVE GROUP

In the first two chapters of this introductory unit we examined the aspects of the definition of group decision making and the conditions under which group decision making is most appropriate. In the third chapter, we turn our attention to the criteria of an effective group. Since learning group decision-making skills can only be accomplished by working in groups, and since group work will begin early in a term whether or not the basic skills have been studied, it is useful to examine guidelines that you can use to monitor your group efforts. As you begin deliberations, you may well find that your group immediately meets some of these criteria. When your group encounters difficulty, you may find that your understanding of these guidelines will point out the areas in which your group needs work.

Summaries of group research by Hare[1] and Shaw[2] list many elements that effective groups have in common. The seven criteria we offer in this profile conform to the key elements in these and similar lists. Although a group can produce a good decision without necessarily meeting each of the following criteria fully, neglect or absence of one or more not only seriously hampers a group's efforts in achieving the best decision but is disruptive to the interpersonal relations of the group's members.

An effective group will most likely be a product of the following:

1. An environment that promotes group interaction.

2. Optimum size.

3. Functioning as a cohesive unit.

4. A commitment to a specific task.

5. Norms that help a group to work.

6. People who have enough expertise and aggregate skills to meet key role requirements.

7. Free interaction to reach a decision.

Let's consider each of these criteria separately.

---

[1] A. Paul Hare, *Handbook of Small Group Research* 2nd ed. (New York: Free Press, 1976), pp. 331–355.
[2] Marvin E. Shaw, *Group Dynamics* 3rd ed. (New York: McGraw-Hill, 1981), pp. 391–399.

Environment

An effective group works in an environment that promotes group interaction. The work environment has both a physical and a psychological dimension. The physical dimension includes room temperature, lighting, and seating arrangements.

The importance of comfortable room temperature and adequate lighting are self-evident. Group members will not behave effectively if they are too warm or too cold or if lighting is too dim or too glaring. By far the most important consideration is the seating.

Too often, seating is too formal or too informal for the best interaction. By too formal, I mean a board-of-directors seating style. Imagine the long polished oak table with the chairperson at the head, the leading lieutenants at right and left, and the rest of the people down the line, as illustrated in Figure 3-1(a). Seating is an indication of status. Thus, how the seating is arranged can facilitate or kill real and total interaction. In the board of directors seating style, a "boss-and-subordinate" pattern emerges. People are unlikely to speak until they are asked to do so. Moreover, no one has a good view of all the people present.

On the other hand, an excessively informal setting may also inhibit interaction. In an informal arrangement, people just sit where they can be most comfortable. In Figure 3-1(b), three people sitting on the couch form their own little group; the two seated next to each other form another group. Two members have placed themselves out of the main flow. The group interaction will be casual, but it may not be the most effective.

The ideal arrangement is the circle, represented by Figure 3-1(c). Here everyone can see everyone else. At least physically, everyone has equal status. If the meeting place does not have a round table, you may be better off without a table or with an arrangement of tables that make a square, as in Figure 3-1(d), which approximates the circle arrangement.

The advantages of the circle are that sight lines are better and motivation to speak is higher. At an oblong table, for example, those at the ends will be perceived as having higher status—they will be deferred to as leaders. Those sitting on the corners will tend to speak less than those on the ends or in the middle.

When the group is presenting information to an audience, the group members should sit in a semicircle facing the audience so they can see the audience and other members of the group at the same time.

Once a group begins its deliberations, the value of an effective physical environment will probably not be noticed or talked about. But if a group is in an uncomfortable or inappropriate physical setting, it may well lose its potential for effectiveness.

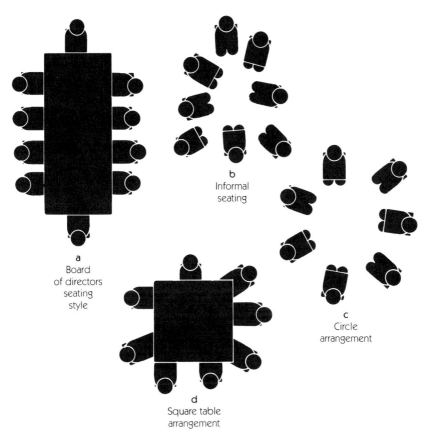

a
Board
of directors
seating
style

b
Informal
seating

c
Circle
arrangement

d
Square table
arrangement

Figure 3-1. Seating arrangements.

As you can see, the physical dimension lays the groundwork for the psychological dimension, the climate for discussion.

From the beginning, it is important for the group to establish a climate that allows each person to participate. Anything that suggests that only one person is to be listened to or that some persons have ideas that are generally unworthy will hurt the group's efforts to achieve a balance of participation. People will not participate if they fear personal attack or if they feel unable to protect themselves from the attacks of others. If people believe that their ideas will be belittled, ridiculed, or discounted or that no one will intervene to allow their ideas to be heard, the chance for total interaction is destroyed.

As a group deliberates, certain individuals will earn higher status than others. In a particular subject area, for instance, one person may be acknowledged as having better information, greater insight, or a more logical perspective. As a result, that person's comments will carry more weight in that area.

But an effective group provides a climate where everyone has equal opportunity to earn higher status.

EXERCISES

Select for analysis one of the most recent decision-making groups you have worked with. Each exercise in this chapter calls for examination of the group from a different standpoint in order to increase your awareness of the importance of each criterion of group effectiveness.

1. ◆ What was the physical environment of the group? Comment on seating arrangement (around a table? in a circle? scattered?), kinds of chairs, temperature, lighting, and so forth.

2. ◆ What was the psychological environment for the group? Comment on the actual or perceived status of members, respect for thoughts of participants, and encouragement of contribution.

3. ◆ What effect, if any, did the environment have on the communication? On the decision?

Optimum Size

Whether or not a group can work effectively may well be a function of size. Conventional wisdom dictates that "bigger is better." As a result, when people examine major problems facing society, they almost always create large bodies. But large groups are seldom effective; many people cannot or will not contribute, cohesiveness is nearly impossible to develop, and the decision is seldom a product of the group's collective thought.

What is the ideal size of a decision-making group? Most research finds that optimum size depends on the nature of the task. Yet five-person groups are considered ideal by many.[3] Why five? Groups with fewer than five members almost universally complain that they are too small and that there are not enough people for specialization. To be effective, a group needs certain skills. When the group contains only three or four members, chances are small that these skills will be present. Moreover, if one member of a group of three does not feel like contributing, you no longer have much of a group.

Nevertheless, in many settings the three-person group is a common prac-

[3] Hare, p. 214.

tice. It's easier to get three people together than five or more. And if the task is relatively simple or within the expertise of the individuals, the three-person group may be a good choice. A good guideline to follow is: the three-person group will work when the people are members of relatively small homogeneous bodies. Department faculties for example, range from nine to fifteen, and the faculty committees are thus likely to contain no more than three people.

It has also been found that when a group numbers more than seven or eight, reticent members are even less likely to contribute. As the group grows larger, two, three, or four people may become the central spokespersons, with others playing more passive roles.[4]

Just as there are conditions under which the three-person group may be the best, so there are circumstances where a group of ten, eighteen, or even thirty *might* be good. A larger group is good when the plan calls for several smaller decision-making groups. For instance, if a university committee of twenty-six is formed to consider the question of what the university's participation, if any, should be in the process of selecting and using cable television, the large group might well be subdivided into three groups. One group might deal with the issues of responding to cable company bids, one might examine the programming potential of the university, and a third might determine contractual matters.

In a group of any size, an odd number is better than an even number. Why? Although voting is not the best way of reaching a decision, if a group finds it necessary to resolve an issue on which it cannot achieve consensus, the odd number will prevent tie votes.

EXERCISES

1. ◆ How large was your group?

2. ◆ What was the relationship between size and communication? Between size and the quality of the decision?

Cohesiveness

An extremely important prerequisite of an effective decision-making group is its potential for cohesiveness. Remember the three musketeers who were all for one and one for all? They are the prototype of a cohesive group. Cohesive-

[4]Shaw, p. 202.

ness means sticking together, pulling for each other, and being caught up in the task.

What determines the potential for group cohesiveness? At least three qualities seem particularly important. First is the attractiveness of the group's purpose. Members identify with each other when the group's goals are particularly appealing. Social or fraternal groups, for example, build cohesiveness out of devotion to brotherhood or service. In a decision-making group, attractiveness is likely to be related to how important the task is to members. Suppose a department forms a committee to consider how its curriculum can be made more responsive to student needs. The cohesiveness of the members of that committee will rely, at least in part, on the importance they attribute to this issue.

A second important quality necessary for cohesiveness is similarity of the needs and interests of members. Groups may be characterized as homogeneous or heterogeneous. A homogeneous group is one in which members have a great deal in common. For example, a group of five women of the same age who are all strong feminists would be homogeneous. A heterogeneous group is one in which various ages, knowledge, attitudes, and interests are represented. A homogeneous group is likely to achieve cohesiveness more quickly than a heterogeneous group because the members are more likely to identify with each other's needs and interests from the start.

If a department has three divisions (communication, theater, and speech therapy, for example), a committee of faculty or students drawn from all three divisions may have more difficulty developing cohesiveness than a committee of faculty or students drawn from only one of the divisions. On the other hand, the committee drawn from three divisions is likely to be more cohesive than a committee drawn from separate departments in a college. I am not arguing for total homogeneity. A group needs some heterogeneity to ensure differing viewpoints and experiences. But a too-diverse group runs the risk of failing to achieve necessary cohesiveness.

A third important quality is reinforcement of interpersonal needs. William Schutz has identified affection (showing affection to others and receiving affection from others), inclusion (including others in activities and being included by others in their activities), and control (having a role in determining what will happen) as major interpersonal needs.[5] Group cohesion seems directly related to the belief of individual members that they are liked, included, and respected. As people decide they like each other, that they want to be around each other, and that their opinions will be respected, they begin to

[5]William Schutz, *The Interpersonal Underworld* (Palo Alto, Calif.: Science & Behavior Books, 1966), pp. 18–20.

work more effectively as a unit.

Cohesiveness is difficult to develop in a one-meeting group. It is and should be characteristic of ongoing groups. It is usually generated after initial meetings and should be well established during or before the group reaches its most productive stages.

EXERCISES

1. Discuss the factors that affect cohesiveness: attractiveness of the group's goals, similarity of needs and interests, and reinforcement of interpersonal needs.

2. What effect did presence or absence of these factors have on communication in your group? On the quality of the decisions reached?

Commitment to Task

Another prerequisite of an effective group is its commitment to the task—its desire to accomplish the goal. A decision-making group convenes as a result of the need to arrive at a decision. Completion of the task is the primary goal that the decision-making group shares, and how effectively the group functions often depends on the commitment the membership has to that particular task. Whether the task is assigned to the group or whether the group itself determines its task, members of the group must have a commitment to task completion.

When someone appoints you to a committee or asks you to serve on one, you have to decide whether you want to be a part of that decision-making group. You are occasionally assigned to a decision-making group (or are asked by a superior in such a way that declining is difficult), but you usually have the option of saying no. You must be honest with yourself and with your superiors when you have a choice. Group membership implies commitment, and you will be treated as if you are committed. If you join a group because you can't refuse the person who asked you or because the people in the group are people you like to be with, you might be making a big mistake. Sometimes a sense of commitment develops as the group proceeds with its work, but unless some sense of commitment is shown by members, the group will probably have difficulty functioning. Too often after a person has become a part of a group, he or she realizes the mistake—but then feels it is too late to get out. Often the person misses meetings, avoids work, and just doesn't do a good job. Such behavior is not helpful to anyone in the group.

Of course, commitment to task is often directly related to the clarity and perceived importance of the task. If the group goal is ambiguous or is perceived to be of little importance, individual commitment is likely to be weak. Because of its importance to both member commitment and procedure, determining the group goal is the subject of the entire next chapter.

EXERCISES

1. ◆ In the most recent group you worked with, what sense of commitment did you have for the task? What, in your opinion, was the sense of commitment of other group members?

2. ◆ What effect did the commitment to task (or lack of it) have on communication? On the quality of the decision?

Developing Norms

An effective group develops norms that help the group work. *Norms* are the guidelines for behavior that are established or are perceived to be established for conducting group business, and are the most powerful determiners of behavior in groups. In this section we will explore how norms develop, how they affect member behavior, and how you can help your group form appropriate norms.

Norms begin to be established at the onset of a group's deliberations. They grow, change, and solidify as people get to know one another better.

Norms for a group may be formally spelled out in a group's operating guidelines (such as in parliamentary procedures for organizational meetings), they may be adapted from proven social guidelines (such as "Don't talk about yourself in a decision-making group meeting"), or they may simply develop within a particular context. For instance, without previous discussion, the members of a given group may refrain from using common four-letter words during the meeting. When business has ended, conversation may become more earthy.

Although formally stated norms may be known to you from the beginning, most group norms are learned through experience with a specific group, and because norms may vary from one group to the next, we have to relearn them. Two particularly important areas of norm development are in group interaction and group procedure. In one group it may be all right to interrupt any speaker at any time; in another, no one may speak until he or she is recognized. Thus, Martha, who is used to raising her hand to be recognized at the business meetings of her social organization, may find herself unable to speak in a group meeting where the participants break in whenever they have a chance. In one group it may be all right for someone to openly express anger or hostility toward a person or an idea; in another group, anger and hostility are never allowed to surface. In one group, member status may determine who speaks first, longest, or most often, while in another group, member status may have no effect on interaction.

The second area in which norm development is particularly important is in group procedure. In one group, it may be accepted that people will come and go as they please; in another group business does not start until everyone is present, and the group stops its work when someone has to leave. In one group, members may socialize for a few minutes, exchanging greetings or inquiring about family or activities; in another group, members may move directly to the task at hand. In one group, members may sit in a definite, predetermined spatial arrangement; in another group, members may sit where they feel most comfortable.

Norms help a group develop cohesiveness. As members conform to stated or implied guidelines of behavior, they find themselves relating to each other more effectively. One of the initial hurdles group members must surmount is called *primary tension,* the anxieties of getting to know each other. As group members test out verbal and nonverbal behavior to see what will be accepted, they begin to become more comfortable with each other, primary tension is lessened, and the group is able to concentrate on its task.

As you begin work in a group, you should be very conscious of what norms seem to be in operation and whether or not those norms will help the group's work. If you believe that certain norms are detrimental or destructive, you will need to make your position and the reasons for that position known. For if you do not, those norms can become established. Once norms are established and reinforced, they are very difficult to change.

How can norms be detrimental or destructive? Let us consider a hypothetical situation. Paul is a member of a group formed to consider dress codes for new employees. At the beginning of the first meeting, a few members of the group tell jokes and generally have a good time. If such behavior is allowed or encouraged, cutting up, making light of the task, and joke telling become a group norm. As a result, the group may get so engaged in these behaviors that the task is delayed, set aside, or perhaps even forgotten. Participants may describe their experience by saying. "We don't do much, but it's fun." Others may be very concerned with such behavior, but if it goes on for several meetings, it will be very hard to change. As a result of the norms that are developed, the group is likely to waste a great deal of time. In fact, the group may not be able to make the kinds of decisions that were expected.

What happens when norms are violated? A person who does not go along with developing norms may be ignored, his words may be discounted, and he may even be punished by the group. For instance, in the fun-loving group described above, if a person is appointed to a committee after the group has held several meetings, and if he or she attempts to get down to business early in the meeting, he or or she is very likely to be ignored. It is even more likely that the group will look on the person as a company man or a spoilsport, and his words will be greeted with a certain amount of contempt or hostility. The more cohesive a group becomes, the more pronounced will be the pressure to adhere to group norms.

As you examine a group's decision making, you may well find that the group's norms have contributed to or detracted from its productivity.

So, what can you do in your group? If you are a member of a group at its formation, you may be instrumental in developing its norms; if you join a group after it has met several times, how well you recognize and conform to the established norms may well determine your potential influence on the group.

Before the group even begins, you can make a mental assessment of group goals and determine the kinds of norms that are most appropriate for that group in achieving those goals. Then, as the group begins, you can behave according to the norms and make statements that will be in line with those behaviors. If you act as a role model, others may pick up your cues and conform; the likelihood that conformity will occur depends on many variables including your perceived status in the group. If the group seems to be establishing norms that are counter to what is appropriate, you can speak early in the group meeting to tell why certain behaviors seem to be important. You may not, of course, be able to establish the norms you think are best, but if you make an effort, and if that effort is seen as constructive, there is a good chance that you will be at least partially successful.

Note that norms can be established even though members are not aware of the process. For instance, after a group has met four or five times, if you were to ask the group "What are your norms?" there is a very real chance that they will respond with, "We don't have any." Yet, if you are truly aware of what norms are and if you remain alert, you can see norms emerging—you will see some being rejected and some being entrenched. Most important, you will see that the norms will affect the end product far more than participants are likely to recognize.

EXERCISES

1. ♦ Try to determine the norms that operated in your decision-making group. Had the norms always been the same? Or had they evolved over a period of time?

2. ♦ What happened to a person who violated the group's norms? In what ways did recognition of norms help the group to function more effectively?

Meeting Key Role Requirements

To operate effectively, the members of the group must want to play, or have a potential for playing, the roles that accomplish basic task and maintenance functions.

A *role* is a pattern of behavior that characterizes an individual's place in a group. In an effective decision-making group, the major roles necessary for accomplishing the task are played by the group members. In groups, role specialization is likely to occur; that is, people will play the roles that are suited to them or that they are asked to play. Members of the group accept people for the roles they play, or influence people to play other roles. Members are also likely to agree on the status or importance of each of the roles in helping to achieve the goal.

When you join a group, you look for clues to direct your behavior. Whether you recognize it or not, you make systematic decisions to behave in a given way within a group. What determines how you behave? What roles do you assume? Some of your choices are made on the basis of group norms that have been established. Other choices are determined by your perceptions of yourself and by the feedback you get from others.

To a great extent, your personality will affect your group behavior. A quiet person will not behave the same way an aggressive person behaves; a jovial person will perform a somewhat different role from that of a suspicious person. Your reputation from outside the group will often affect the role you play within a group. However, your behavior may also be a product of how you are treated by others or of what others expect your behavior to be. If others want you to be a clown, you may well live up to that role; if others look to you for leadership, you may provide it even though you did not plan to take on a leadership role.

The roles you play become productive when they complement the functions a group serves. All decision-making groups have two clearly definable functions. The first is task. The *task function* includes all the work a group must do to accomplish the group goal. Thus, if the group goal is to determine

college entrance requirements, the group must find information about requirements, determine a procedure for best using the information, decide what
must be accomplished at various places in the discussion, keep the group on
the subject (at least most of the time), and so forth. Although nearly everyone
in the group should and will provide information, some may show themselves
to be better at testing information, some at asking the right questions, some at
putting information into perspective, and some at determining consequences
of behavior.

The second function, the *maintenance function,* is related to keeping the
group working together smoothly. The maintenance function facilitates cohesion and good interpersonal and working relationships. Some people are best
at drawing out individuals, harmonizing conflicts, or saying things that make
members feel good about working with each other.

The major roles in a group, then, may be classified as task-oriented roles
or maintenance-oriented roles. Both kinds must be present for a group to
arrive at good decisions that are supported by all members. Of course, not all
roles played in a group are positive. By accident, or occasionally by design,
people say and do things that hurt the group's ability to work together. Thus,
helping people to play positive roles is an important factor in any group.

Group members often perceive the most important role in the group to be
that of the leader. The leader is designated by outside authority, is appointed
or elected by the group, or takes over leadership responsibilities in the group
for a given period of time. The leader's role is to exert influence toward
attaining group goals and maintaining group interpersonal needs. The role of
leader is not one role, but a combination of many task and maintenance roles.
Leadership, as we will see later, is not solely the province of the leader.
Nearly every role played contributes to the leadership of a group, but the
leader may well be the one who plays certain task or maintenance roles most
competently.

Let us look at several task and maintenance functions that need to be met
in the group. Keep in mind that one individual might be able to fulfill four or
five of the roles and another individual only one or two. Since the skills
necessary to play these roles are discussed in various parts of the book, I will
indicate where the skills necessary for playing the role are presented as I
define each role.

In most group discussions there are at least four major task roles that can
be identified: information-giver, clarifier, expediter, and analyzer.

Information Giver or Opinion Giver   Information-giving and opinion-giving
provide content for the discussion; about 50 percent of all that is done in a
group can be labeled information-giving or opinion-giving. Without informa-

tion, the group will not have the material necessary to make decisions. Everyone in the group plays the information-giving role during discussion, but there are usually one or more persons who have *really* done their homework. Although some groups rely on a designated resource person or a consultant to fulfill the information-giving role, in most groups it's the responsibility of every person to be well prepared. Chapter 6, "Researching the Question," will consider the skills of solid preparation; Chapter 7, "Discussing the Question," considers several specific skills of information-giving.

Clarifier   The clarifier plays the role of ensuring that the group understands ideas and feelings. At times, the clarifier will ask questions to get members to reveal data necessary to clarify meaning; at other times the clarifier will paraphrase information to test understanding of ideas and feelings. More than one person will play the clarifier role during the discussion, but there are usually only one or two members of the group who are especially adept at these skills. A good clarifier is indispensible to the group. Chapter 7 will discuss the skills of questioning and paraphrasing.

Expediter   The expediter perceives when the group is going astray and says something to help get the group back on track. Groups will get sidetracked, and sometimes apparent digressions are necessary to get background, to enlarge the scope, or even to give a person an opportunity to get something off his chest. But these digressions may take the group far afield. Every group needs someone who can gracefully play the expediter role. Chapter 5, "Analyzing the Question," provides the information necessary to effectively play the role of expediter.

Analyzer   Analyzers are masters of technique. Analyzers know which subquestions must be considered in order for the group to reach a rational decision. They know when the group skips a point, passes over a point too lightly, or is not taking a look at important matters. In addition, analyzers examine the reasoning of the group. The skills of expediting and analyzing go hand in hand. Chapter 5, "Analyzing the Question," presents the information that is vital for expediting and analyzing. The tests that the analyzer applies to evidence and reasoning are discussed in Chapter 9, "Drawing Conclusions in Groups."

Now that we have looked at the roles that facilitate accomplishing the task, let us consider the major roles in facilitating good interpersonal relations. The major maintenance roles are supporter, gatekeeper, harmonizer, and tension reliever.

Supporter   People in groups are likely to feel better about their participation when their thoughts and feelings are recognized; members who recognize and validate a person's right to speak are playing the role of supporter. In any group we expect everyone to give support at some time, but people tend to get so wrapped up in their own ideas that they may neglect to reward the positive comments that are made. The supporter responds verbally or nonverbally whenever a good point is made. Support skills will be considered in Chapter 7.

Gatekeeper   The gatekeeper is the person who helps to keep communication channels open. If a group has seven people, the assumption is that all seven have something to contribute. But if all are to feel comfortable in contributing, those who tend to dominate need to be held in check and those who tend to be reticent need to be encouraged. The gatekeeper is the one who sees that Jane is on the edge of her chair, ready to talk, but just cannot seem to get in, that Don is rambling a bit and needs to be directed, that Tom's need to talk so frequently is making Cesar withdraw from the conversation, or that Betty has just lost the thread of discussion. The important role of gatekeeping will be considered in Chapter 7, "Discussing the Question."

Harmonizer   Since it is a rare group that can expect to accomplish its task without some minor, if not major, conflicts, there is always need for a harmonizer. The harmonizer is responsible for reducing and reconciling misunderstandings, disagreements, and conflicts. The harmonizer encourages objectivity and mediates between hostile, aggressively competing sides. How the harmonizer proceeds is discussed in Chapter 8, "Managing Conflict in Groups."

Tension Reliever   Folklore has it that "all work and no play makes Jack a dull boy." When group members really work on their tasks, they sometimes get so involved and try so hard that they begin to wear themselves down. Nerves get frayed, vision becomes cloudy, and the machine of progress grinds to a halt. The tension reliever is the person who recognizes when the process is boring or when the group is getting tired. He has a sixth sense for when to tell a joke, when to digress, or when to get the group to play a little before returning to the task. In some situations, a single well-placed sentence will get a laugh, break the monotony, and jolt the group out of their lethargy. At other times, the group can be saved only with a real break—sometimes a minute or so or even five, ten, or fifteen minutes. Of all the roles we have discussed, this is the hardest to play consciously. If someone tries to be a tension-reliever, he will usually fail. Although not every group has a member who fills the bill completely, groups include at least one person who can play tension reliever enough to get the group through tough moments.

EXERCISES

1.♦ In the most recent group you worked with, what roles do you perceive as having been well represented by group members? Underrepresented?

2.♦ What effect did representation or underrepresentation of roles have on communication? On quality of the decision?

Interaction

An effective group is one that reaches conclusions through the interaction of its members. Not only must each member of the group be well prepared by having gathered information, analyzed the question, and considered the possible choices, but each person must be willing to contribute to the group decision. If a decision is not a product of group thought and group interaction, the advantages of group decision making are lost.

When a leader has too much authority, a group runs the risk of having its decisions made by decree. For example, after the group discussion, the leader tells group what its decision will be. If the leader has enough power, is very persuasive, or is very manipulative, he can get the group to approve a decision. This method, called rubber-stamping, often destroys group decision making and group morale.

Group members often feel more pleased about the process and more committed to the group decisions when such decisions are reached democratically through group interaction. Democratic decision making is reached by consensus. *Consensus* means total group agreement. After the group has discussed a point for a while, the leader poses a question that is phrased to capture the essence of the group's position. For example, after the group had been discussing departmental problems for a while the leader might ask the question, ''Are we in agreement that lack of direction is frustrating the efforts of department members?'' If everyone agrees, the decision is reached by consensus.

If the group does not agree, the group continues to discuss the point until a statement can be made that incorporates divergent viewpoints without compromising the principles behind the viewpoints. But it takes the participation of most group members to arrive at a statement that represents the group position.

If consensus still cannot be reached, the group usually takes a vote. Let us say that after considerable discussion on determining a major cause of department frustration, it becomes obvious that no single statement can be made that will be satisfactory to all. The group should then take a vote. If the vote is six to one or five to two in a seven-person group, the decision has been given solid support. If it is a four-to-three decision, there may be some question about later group support of that decision. Nevertheless, on some issues, at some times, the principle of majority rule is the only choice open.

If a group member sees that only a few members are getting a chance to talk or are making any effort to talk, it is up to that group member to play the role of gatekeeper—to bring the other members of the group. Even if a person is only willing to say that he or she agrees with what someone else has said, the group at least sees that person's position on the issue.

So far we have focused on the necessity of full participation and consensus if possible. Now let us consider how we can determine whether the interaction has been worthwhile. To do so we must examine the decision-making process. Evaluation of group interaction ultimately focuses on four areas: clarity of goal, pursuance of key issues, quality of information, and documentation of process.

First, did the group have a clearly defined goal? A decision-making group is formed because one or more persons see the need for a decision: a need to determine the facts, to evaluate, or to suggest a course of action. The specific phrasing for the topic question, however, is often left up to the group. For instance, a group may be formed to discuss fees. It is up to the group to crystallize its goal into a topic question such as "What fee level is necessary to ensure income for the organization?" or "What should the fee level be for next year?" The group will spend a certain amount of its time determining its specific goal. If the group's goal is never really made clear, it is unlikely that the group will arrive at a good decision.

Second, did the group follow a logical procedure? Although groups rarely move in a well-organized manner through a series of steps, effective decision-making groups should eventually consider the key subquestions that must be resolved to produce a logical decision. How well group members are able to analyze their question to reveal the key subquestions will to a large extent determine whether the group's procedure is logical.

Third, did the group base its decision on good material? Good decisions are informed decisions. Groups can rarely rely on intuition, emotion, or speculation and expect to be successful. A group that wants to ensure a high probability of success must gather the best possible information on the topic. Every person in the group bears the responsibility for finding good information.

Fourth, did the group document its procedure? As we will discuss later, every group should have a written record of what took place. An outline of the process should accompany the group's decision. When the procedure is documented, the parent organization, as well as the critic, can satisfy itself that decisions have been carefully made. Without a written record (unless you observe the group in action), there is no adequate means for testing the group's process.

EXERCISES

1. In the most recent group you worked with, did everyone participate in the group decision making? How did participation or lack of it affect the quality of the decision making?

2. Did your group interact to achieve group consensus or were decisions made by decree and then rubber-stamped? What was the effect of the method of decision making?

3. Did the group have a clear goal? Did the group determine a logical procedure? Were group members well prepared? Was the interaction documented?

Summary

An ideal group can be identified by seven characteristics. The effective group works in a physical and psychological setting that facilitates good interaction. Not only must temperature, lighting, and seating arrangements be considered, but each person must feel that he or she has the right to contribute and to be taken seriously.

The effective group is of optimum size. For most groups this means approximately five members. However, optimum size depends on the nature of the task and the skills of the members.

The effective group functions as a cohesive unit. At least three qualities seem particularly important in contributing to group cohesiveness: attractiveness of group goals, similarity of the needs and interests of the members, and an atmosphere of reinforcement of interpersonal needs.

The effective group shows a commitment to its specific task. Members of such a group want to be a part of that group and are willing to work to make it a success.

The effective group develops norms that help the group work. Norms grow, change, and solidify as the people in the group get to know one another. Norms are particularly important in determining group interaction and group procedures.

The effective group contains people who have enough expertise and aggregate skills to meet key role requirements. The roles that members of a group play become productive when they meet task and maintenance functions. The task function includes all the work a group must do to accomplish the goal. The maintenance function includes all the things that facilitate cohesion and good interpersonal and working relationships.

The effective group interacts freely to reach a good decision. Although the quality of a decision may not be discovered until long after the decision is implemented, a group's decision may still be evaluated on the basis of the group's process.

Readings for Part One

The following are valuable current sources of research findings in group communication.

Cragan, John F., and Wright, David W. "Small Group Communication Research of the 1970's: A Synthesis and Critique." *Central States Speech Journal,* Vol. 31 (Fall 1980). An excellent bibliography of research appearing in major communication journals.

Hare, A. Paul. *Handbook of Small Group Research,* 2nd ed. New York: The Free Press, 1976. In addition to more than 400 pages of review of the literature, Hare cites 6032 studies in his more than 300-page bibliography.

Shaw, Marvin E. *Group Dynamics: The Psychology of Small Group Behavior,* 3rd ed. New York: McGraw-Hill, 1981. Perhaps the best discussion of research findings available.

TWO

THE GROUP
DECISION-MAKING PROCESS

Group members go through various processes—some processes in preparation for participation, and others during group interaction—in order to arrive at the best possible decision. In this unit you will learn to write and test the topic question, analyze the question, research the question, master essential group communication skills, cope with conflict, apply supplemental approaches to decision making, and draw sound group conclusions.

4

DETERMINING THE GROUP'S GOAL

Your group will, of course, have some idea of why it is meeting. Under ideal circumstances the chairperson of the parent group or the manager of the organization of which you are a member will have presented your group with a topic phrased well enough to define your goal. Many times, however, you and your group will have to do the defining. For instance, your group may be created to decide a clearly phrased goal such as, "determine the effects of the return to walking a beat on community-police relations in the Third Precinct." It is much more likely, however, that your group would be presented with a general goal such as "to look into community relations in the Third Precinct" or vaguer yet, "to look at how things are going in the Third Precinct." Often, the first job of the group will be to determine a specific goal that is in congruence with the goal of the organization. Given a vague goal, a group that does not know how to proceed can end up spending a disproportionate amount of time deciding what it is supposed to do. And as I have already pointed out, the greater the group ambiguity about the goal, the less group satisfaction and commitment and the reduced likelihood of a "good" decision.

What is evidence of a well-conceived group goal? How is a vaguely worded group goal crystallized into a workable sentence? The remainder of this chapter answers these questions. We will consider (1) wording the group goal as a question, (2) ramifications of different types of questions, (3) selecting the appropriate question, and (4) criteria for testing wording.

Writing the Group Goal as a Question

The goal for decision-making groups should be written as a question. Why a question? First, a well-written question will not reflect any particular bias; moreover, a question is a sentence designed to elicit a response. Because the goal of discussion is to stimulate group consideration, the problem itself, and all subheadings for that matter, should be phrased as questions.

Let us consider two examples to illustrate group procedure. Suppose a group is formed to make a recommendation for improving department productivity. Members of the group might suggest the following questions to capture the sense of the group's goal:

What can X Corporation do to increase productivity?

What should X Corporation do to increase its productivity?

Can X Corporation increase its productivity to a level that exceeds that of Y Corporation?

Suppose a different group is formed to "look into the way the department advises students about majors." Members of this group might suggest some of the following questions to help define the potential group goal:

What are the current procedures for advising students about majors?

What can the department do to improve counseling for students about majors?

Should the present department procedure for counseling students be modified?

It isn't until a group has written specific questions that it can begin to determine the phrasings that best reflect the group's goal.

Although your group may be presented with such a clear goal that the group need not go through this procedure, it is likely that the group will start with an idea that must be transformed into a clearly stated goal.

Types of Questions

As you work on phrasing the group goal, you will see that the question you choose will fall under one of three headings: questions of fact, questions of evaluation, and questions of policy. Since the type of question not only represents the goal but determines the procedure for arriving at a decision, we will carefully define the three types individually.

Questions of Fact

Questions of fact determine what *is*. Implied in a question of fact is the possibility of determining the facts by direct observation or by spoken or recorded evidence. Questions of fact are asked to classify, to provide descriptive judgment, and to predict. "What are the goals of the Republican party?" is a question of *classification*. Goals can be determined and verified. "Is Jones guilty of shoplifting?" is a question of *descriptive judgment*. Jones either committed the crime or he did not. "Will the economy improve enough to provide a favorable sales climate?" is a question of prediction. It seeks to determine what will be factual in the future.

Deciding questions of fact is likely to be the goal of fact-finding commissions, research groups, governmental committees, and juries.

Questions of Evaluation

Questions of evaluation consider relative goodness or badness. They are characterized by evaluative words such as "effective," "good," "worthy," "better," or their opposites. The goal of the question of evaluation is to compare a subject with one or more members of the same classification. "What is the best cable television system for the city of Cincinnati?" is a question of evaluation that various citizens' committees were asked to decide. "Are graduates with an associate degree more valuable to our firm than graduates with a bachelor's degree?" is a question of evaluation that a personnel policy review team might have to consider.

We can set up criteria for "best" and "more valuable" and measure our possible choices against those criteria, but there is no way of verifying our findings—the answer is still a matter of judgment, not a matter of fact. Although questions of evaluation may be the ultimate goal of some decision-making groups, what you are likely to find is that one or more questions of evaluation must be resolved as questions of policy, our last category for consideration.

Questions of Policy

Questions of policy ask what action should be taken. A question of policy is phrased: (1) to arrive at a solution to a problem, (2) to test a tentative solution to a felt need, or (3) to pick from possible actions. "What should we do to lower the rate of theft among employees?" is a question that requires a group to decide what actions should be taken in order to deal with the problem of the increase in the rate of employee theft. "Should budget cuts be absorbed equally by all departments?" tests the feasibility of a proposed solution. "How should this business meet federal affirmative action goals?" asks a group to determine a feasible plan that can be followed from among those offered. The inclusion of the word "should" in most questions of policy makes them the easiest to recognize and the easiest to phrase of all decision-making questions. By far the greatest number of questions facing decision-making groups in the real world are questions of policy.

Selecting the Appropriate Question

In the last section we defined the three major types of questions, but definition alone does not give you a solid rationale for making the most appropriate choice. To make a sound choice, you must understand the implications of each type of question.

Taking a comparative approach to each of the three types of questions, let us suppose that the group has been given the general goal of exploring the campus parking problem. Three well-written questions that relate to this problem area are:

What can be done to reduce the parking problem on campus?

What are the best plans for reducing the campus parking problem?

What should the administration do to reduce the campus parking problem?

Each of these is phrased well enough to direct a decision-making group. On the surface the three questions look quite similar—they explore the same subject area and seem only marginally different. Are they essentially the same? Even though each speaks about the same goal—exploring the campus parking problem—the three differ significantly in determining group goals.

Let's look closely at the operative words in each question. The first question focuses on *what can be done;* the second focuses on *what plans are the best;* and the third focuses on *what should be done*—a choice of plans. Informal discussions of each of the three questions may be quite similar. But group decision making is not informal discussion; group decision making is a process designed to achieve a goal that best meets the needs of the group. The significance of the three questions as written is that each asks for a different *type* of decision.

When we ask, "What can be done?" we are seeking a list of possible procedures—a list of alternatives. What will happen to that list? Who knows? The group will complete its task when it has decided that it has listed all the possible ways for reducing campus parking problems.

Even a question such as "Is Jones guilty of shoplifting?" asks only for the facts—enough facts to render a decision. The group is not asked to deal with value judgments, such as whether shoplifting is a major crime or a minor crime. Neither is the group asked to determine what should be done with Jones as a result of his guilt or innocence.

Phrasing the goal of the group as a question of fact is appropriate when the group sees its task primarily as one of information gathering. Whether the phrasing asks, "What can be done?" "What is the truth?" "What are the facts?" "Is a behavior labeled by a certain term?" all are questions of fact, and all are appropriate as information gathering goals.

The question "What are the best plans for reducing the campus parking problem?" is a question of evaluation. When we ask, "What are the best?" we are looking for more than just a listing of alternatives. With this phrasing, the group must evaluate each alternative in order to determine which one or ones of the many possible plans are the best. Will one of the appropriate plans be put into action? Again, our answer is "Who knows?" The group completes its task when it has decided which plan or plans the group considers best and has recommended the results to whoever must make a decision.

When should you accept a question of evaluation for the appropriate phrasing of the group goal? When you see your job as one of comparison. Sometimes the comparison is with some arbitrary standard that the group will determine. "What are the best plans for reducing the campus parking problem?" calls for the group to compare the various plans on the basis of what is best. Sometimes the comparison is between two or more choices. In this case the choices are compared on the basis of a standard. "Are graduates with an associate degree more valuable to our firm than graduates with a bachelor's degree?" calls for the group to compare the two alternatives on the basis of what is determined to be "more valuable."

"What should the administration do to reduce the campus parking problem?" is a question of policy. When we ask "What should be done?" we are looking for more than a list of alternatives or a determination of what is best. This phrasing calls for the group to determine what action should be taken. Questions of policy put the emphasis on action and are especially appropriate when the group has the authority to act itself. Even groups such as advisory boards with no power to act must recommend action when presented with questions of policy.

Effective group decision making requires that the group choose the operative words ("can," "best," "should") with great care. Operative words indicate the kinds of decisions desired, and as we will see throughout this book, each phrasing suggests a different procedure for decision making. So, when you hear someone say, "Let's not worry about the wording of the question, let's get on with the discussion," you should do what you can to convince the group that the wording of the question is imperative if the group is to proceed efficiently and appropriately.

Although the way a question is phrased determines both the nature of the group goal and the method of procedure, all questions are interrelated. If you read the preceding material carefully, you may have noticed a progression. In order to answer one question, a group may have to answer another question first. For example, to answer a question of policy, a group may first have to answer a question of evaluation. To answer a question of evaluation, it may first have to answer a question of fact. In reverse order, a question of fact may lead to a question of evaluation, and a question of evaluation may lead to a question of policy.

EXERCISES

For each of the three sets of discussion questions below, fill in the blanks by changing the wording to conform to the label. In the first set, for example, the question of fact is written. Rewrite the question as one of evaluation and one of policy.

1. Question of fact: "Is Parker selling business secrets to competing firms?"

    Question of evaluation: _____

    Question of policy:_____

2. Question of fact:_____

    Question of evaluation: "Which divisions of the corporation are doing the poorest job in implementing affirmative action programs in their hiring practices?"

    Question of policy: _____

3. Question of fact:_____

    Question of evaluation: _____

    Question of policy: "What should be done to reduce theft in the dormitories?"

Determining Wording

In order to arrive at the wording of a group goal, group members individually and collectively, must go through the following steps:

1. Word the group goal as a question. I have discussed the rationale for stating the goal as a question. Yet even when we know we are supposed to present the goal in question form, it is still possible to overlook this important detail.

2. Word the question clearly enough to identify exactly what the group is to decide. A great danger in any form of communication is to take meaning for granted. We should know enough about the communication process to realize that even when language is clear and explicit, meaning is not necessarily shared. When the question is vague, wordy, and carelessly phrased, confusion is guaranteed. Consider the following questions:

> Should the small basketball games be returned to the university fieldhouse?

> What should the department policy be concerning the courses that aren't getting the job done?

> Should the practices of college service clubs be looked into?

All three questions are well intentioned, and participants in discussions of the questions may have some idea about what they are to decide. But wordings like "small basketball games," "getting the job done," and "looked into" are likely to lead to trouble at some point in the deliberation. Instead of waiting until participants are going in opposite directions in the discussion, it is a good idea to reword questions so that everyone shares the same meaning before the group determines the issues that must be considered. With a bit of work, groups or individuals can learn to produce clearly phrased questions such as:

> Should basketball games with advance ticket sales of less than 5000 be played at the university fieldhouse?

> What should the department policy be concerning those courses that receive low scores on student evaulations?

> Should the university reexamine criteria for selecting membership in college service clubs?

These questions are linguistically superior and give form to the nature of the problem.

3.   Word the question to encourage a spirit of free inquiry. We need to avoid phrasing that subtly or blatantly suggests what the group's decision should be. Consider "Should our ridiculous set of college requirements be revised?" From the start, the group is saddled with a value judgment that should be a result of group deliberation, not a condition for deliberation. Will free inquiry be stimulated when a group has already agreed that requirements are ridiculous? Is the question "Should the country replace highly dangerous nuclear power with clean solar energy?" a good question for discussion? The group should decide whether nuclear power is "Highly dangerous" or whether solar power is "clean". Phrasings that limit the potential for objective analysis should be reworded or eliminated.

4.   Word the question to include only one topic. "Should we ban the internal-combustion engine and replace steel in automobiles with lighter metals and plastics?" contains two related but distinct questions. Both are worthy of consideration—and perhaps both will have to be resolved (along with many other questions) before the auto industry is able to cope with the demands of the future. But they should not be discussed as one topic.

5.   Identify the question as one of fact, evaluation, or policy. How we prepare for and ultimately proceed in the deliberations will be affected by the kind of question we ask. Regardless of how the question is worded, the group

should agree on whether the goal is one of fact finding, evaluation, or policy determination.

6.   Identify wording as open or closed. Whether the question is one of fact, one of evaluation, or one of policy, the group will have to decide whether the question will have open or closed phrasing. Phrasing is *open-ended* when it allows for considerations of many options. *Closed* phrasing offers only one option—it can only be answered yes or no. Contrast the following open and closed questions:

> *Question of fact (open):* Who robbed the M & R Market?
>
> *Question of fact (closed):* Is Jones guilty of robbing the M & R Market?
>
> *Question of evaluation (open):* What is the best cable TV system for the city of Cincinnati?
>
> *Question of evaluation (closed):* Is the Warner Telecommunication Company the best cable TV system for the city of Cincinnati?
>
> *Question of policy (open);* What should the administration do to reduce the campus parking problem?
>
> *Question of policy (closed):* Should the large grass mall in front of the library be turned into a parking lot?

Open questions are most appropriate when considering a total problem area. Closed questions are most appropriate when possibilities have been narrowed to a single choice.

For the most part, an open question is the most appropriate for group decision making because it allows the group to explore all options. Closed questions considerably narrow the scope of the decision making, often too much. Moreover, when the question requires only a yes or a no answer, participants in the process are more likely to choose sides rather than maintain the spirit of inquiry that is most desirable for group decision making.

On the other hand, there are times when closed phrasing is most appropriate. For instance, various citizens' groups may have worked independently on the question of "What company should get the cable television contract for the City of Cincinnati?" If several groups choose Warner Telecommunication, for instance, a subcommittee of the city council might ask: "Should we recommend that the City accept the Warner Telecommunication bid?" A "yes" decision would end the consideration; a "no" decision would reopen consideration of all the companies.

EXERCISES

1.
Label the following questions as (I) open question of fact, (II) closed question of fact, (III) open question of evaluation, (IV) closed question of evaluation, (V) open question of policy, or (VI) closed question of policy.

If the wording of the question meets the tests, place a check mark by it. If there is a problem with wording, indicate the problem by letter and then correct the wording: (A) clarity of focus, (B) discouraging free inquiry, (C) more than one topic, (D) not identifiable as fact, evaluation, or policy.

a. Are American cars inferior to Japanese cars?

b. Whom should we nominate?

c. What are the methods students use to cheat on tests and how can cheating be stopped?

d. How should we cut costs without hurting the quality of the product?

e. What are the five best research studies appearing in recent journals?

2.
Phrase at least three topic questions that seem appropriate for each of the following situations.

a. You have taken several courses in your major. As you examine the curriculum, you are concerned about how the courses fit together to form a program for you. In talking with several other students, you discover that you are not the only one who who has this concern. Moreover, you find that several of your fellow students are willing to join you to examine the relationship among the various courses. Write three topic questions that seem appropriate for group deliberation.

b. As with any business, your company's financial position should fluctuate with the economy. Nevertheless, it has been pointed out that your company's sales records seem to be unrelated to normal economic fluctuations. In fact, even in times of economic upturns your company's sales increase very little. You and four other members of the marketing division are asked to examine the situation. Phrase three topic questions that might be considered by your group.

c. Your boss has put you in charge of the organization's United Appeal fund-raising campaign. Your company's quota is higher this year than last year, yet your organization hasn't met its quota for the last few years. You decide to form a group to analyze the situation. Suggest three topic questions that might be considered for deliberation.

Summary

Determining the group's goal is the first and perhaps the most important step of group decision making.

Determining goals requires the group to understand questions of fact, questions of evaluation, and questions of policy. Questions of fact consider the truth or falsity of an assertion and are most appropriate for groups that see information gathering as their primary goal. Questions of evaluation consider relative goodness or badness. Questions of evaluation are most appropriate for groups that see their primary goal as one of comparison. Questions of policy consider what action should be taken and are appropriate when the group can take action or recommend a course of action.

In wording the group goal, the following guidelines should be considered: (1) the group goal should be a question, (2) the question should be clear, (3) the question should encourage a spirit of free inquiry, (4) the question should include only one topic, (5) the question should be identified as one of fact, evaluation, or policy, and (6) the question should be clearly identified as open or closed.

5

ANALYZING THE QUESTION

As I stated before, group decision making is a process. Almost any process can be subdivided into a series of steps or parts. Whether we are considering a golf swing, writing a book, or, in this case, making a decision, understanding of the parts of the process is necessary for consistent high-quality production. Breaking down or subdividing a process is called *analysis*.

Analysis is a rational procedure; it calls for the individual or the group to sit down, preferably with paper and pencil in hand, and think about a tentative structure or procedure that will result in rational decision making.

As we proceed, you will discover that analysis and research are intertwining processes. As you begin research, you gain the information to begin a basic analysis; as you begin analysis, you discover the areas in which you must do more comprehensive research; and so forth. In this chapter we will consider a basic means of analysis that will enable you to get started on any kind of question.

During your preparation for group work you will be confronted with the question of what portion of the preparation is your individual responsibility and what portion is the group's responsibility. This consideration is especially important when analyzing a question. I advise you to analyze the topic question (the group goal) as soon as the group has determined it and has agreed on the wording. During discussion, the group should share individual analyses and agree on the issues that will serve as guidelines for the group's procedure.

In many groups, the appointed leader will be given the responsibility for determining a tentative agenda based on individual or group analysis. The premise of this chapter is that the group should analyze the question before it begins the major portion of its discussion.

The Search for Issues

The analysis of a question depends on the identification of the issues relevant to that question. Although the word "issue" carries many meanings, decision-making *issues* are the questions whose answers provide information that is vital to the resolution of the topic question. We ask questions because they help us maintain emphasis on the spirit of inquiry. A *vital* question is one that must be considered if the decision is to be a good one.

Suppose you were a member of a group asked to resolve the question "Should the United States increase the amount of money allocated to solar energy research?" Under that topic question, one vital subquestion (issue) is, "Is the amount currently spent insufficient to achieve results?" This subquestion must be asked and answered in order to resolve the topic question. Given a few moments of thought, we are likely to uncover one or more of the key issues under any topic question. In this chapter our goal is to assure ourselves of selecting the major issues. We can uncover the key issues by making a background analysis and a stock issues analysis.

Background Analysis

Any decision-making question exists within a historical context. An analysis of the background enables us to understand this context and may suggest one or more issues that we might not discover in any other way.

History of the Problem

When Santayana said that those who do not study history are bound to repeat it, he verbalized a reality that decision makers must consider. Many of us are inclined to focus on only the immediate aspects of a problem situation. By taking such an approach, however, we may lose vital information and insight. A study of how the problem arose, what attempts have been made to solve it in the past, and why past decisions were or were not good ones will be useful to the current decision-making process.

Consider the energy problem for a moment. A historical analysis can lead us to many periods in our recent past when problems of energy were common, and the student of the energy problem will certainly not ignore the effect of the 1973 oil embargo that triggered a series of decisions about energy. A study of our response to that embargo may well reveal issues that should be considered today.

Immediate Causes of the Problem

The potential problems facing any group or organization are nearly infinite. Why do certain problems seem to need immediate consideration? More often than not, we can identify a trigger incident that made a decision imperative. For example, the Iranian revolution, the ouster of the Shah, and the subsequent battle between Iraq and Iran triggered a new need for emphasis on the energy question in the early 1980s.

Thus, the starting point of our analysis is understanding the background of the problem. This will enable us to see what, if any, historical issues are relevant to today's need for a decision and what has triggered the immediate concern with the problem area. The information from both of these procedures can be considered within the framework of a stock issues analysis.

Stock Issues Analysis

Study of the background provides us with a view of the context in which a decision must be made. Next we need a specific procedure to give structure to the search for issues and to enable us to separate important concerns from lesser concerns. This can be accomplished through the stock issues approach. Although every decision-making context is different—and I cannot emphasize this too much—each can be grouped by the kind of question being asked. A *stock issues analysis* provides a framework for study and for organization based on a universal set of subquestions that can be applied to each question. Because we have identified three kinds of questions (fact, evaluation, and policy), we need to consider three stock issues analyses—one for each type.

The stock issues analysis is not automatic, nor does it take the place of creative thought. But the stock issues analysis is a starting point to suggest questions to uncover specific issues relevant to the particular question being considered.

Let's see how these approaches work.

Questions of Fact

The stock issues analysis of a question of fact includes issues of definition, issues of data, and issues of quality.

A first set of potential issues grows from consideration of definition. As we attempt to determine the facts or whether an alleged fact exists, we must classify the facts. This classification is accomplished through definition. "Did Marshall embezzle department funds?" is a question of fact. Its resolution can only be accomplished after we have defined what is meant by *embezzlement*. Any question of fact will have at least one, and probably several, key terms that must be carefully defined.

Sometimes the definition we need is standardized, as the definition of "voluntary manslaughter" is defined by law in a murder trial. If no standard definition exists or if the standard definition is questionable or not directly applicable to the question, then we must find a workable one. The development or application of that definition will reveal specific key issues.

Another set of issues grows from evidence (data). A question of fact requires the group to seek out the relevant data. If we are considering whether Marshall embezzled funds, we will have to get all the data related to Marshall's behavior at the time in question. But we are not just looking for data at random—we are seeking the data related to the definitions we have previously determined.

A third set of issues grows from considering quality. At times we must consider *extenuating circumstances,* circumstances that may alter perceptions of data discovered. For instance, in determining whether Marshall is guilty of embezzling department funds, we may be in total agreement as to what constitutes embezzlement and we may find evidence that Marshall did commit such a crime. In our investigation, however, we may discover extenuating circumstances that must be considered in addition to the first two issues. For instance, if the embezzlement was done on impulse or as a result of prodding by peers, these circumstances might affect our decision.

Now that we have looked at a rationale for a stock issues approach, let us look at the framework in outline form. Such a framework includes at least the following subquestions:

1. What are the definitions of the key terms? *(issue of definition)*

2. What are the relevant data that satisfy the definition or determine the classifications? *(issue of data)*

3. What extenuating circumstances, if any, affect the decision? *(issue of quality)*

How do we put these broad questions into practice? Ultimately, the choice is the group's—there is no "one and only" way of phrasing the questions. To illustrate the application of this framework, let us consider the three most common types of questions of fact (questions of classification, questions of descriptive judgment, and questions of prediction) with both open and closed phrasings.

Question of Classification

Closed	*Open*
Is "decreasing federal spending" a goal of the Republican party?	What are the goals of the Republican Party?
1. What do we mean by "decreased spending" and "goal"? *(definition)*	1. What do we mean by a party's "goals"? *(definition)*
2. What data determine whether "decreasing spending" is a goal? *(data)*	2. What data determine each of these separate goals? *(data)*
3. What circumstances, if any, override this as a goal? *(quality)*	3. What circumstances, if any, affect or override any of the apparent goals? *(quality)*

Question of Descriptive Judgment

Closed	*Open*
Did Jones murder Smith?	Who murdered Smith?
1. What is meant by "murder"? *(definition)*	1. What is meant by "murder"? *(definition)*
2. Did Jones cause the death of Smith? *(data*—leading to affirmation of Jones's commission of some act)	2. Who are the suspects? *(data)*
	3. Did any of them cause the death of Smith? *(data)*

3. Can Jones's action be defined as "murder"? *(data*—determining whether Jones' action fits the definition)

4. What, if any, extenuating circumstances affect the decision? *(quality)*

4. Can the action of any of the suspects be defined as "murder"? *(data)*

5. What, if any, extenuating circumstances affect the decision? *(quality)*

Question of Prediction

Closed

Will the company be able to absorb the decrease in revenue from the loss of overseas markets?

1. What do we mean by "decrease in revenue" and "loss of overseas markets"? *(definition)*

2. What data are available upon which such a prediction can be made? *(data)*

3. What circumstances, if any, might override the prediction? *(quality)*

Open

What will the company be able to do to absorb the decrease in revenue from the loss of overseas markets?

1. What do we mean by "decrease in revenue" and "loss of overseas markets"? *(definition)*

2. What data are available upon which such a prediction can be made? *(data)*

3. What choices are available? *(data)*

4 What circumstances, if any, might override availability of options? *(quality)*

EXERCISES

Label each of the following questions of fact as (A) a question of classification, (B) a question of descriptive judgment, (C) a question of prediction. Then write a list of appropriate questions based on a stock issues analysis of each.

1. ◆ What criteria can be used by an organization to evaluate cost effectiveness?

2. ◆ What will be the status of the job market for arts and sciences graduates next year?

3. ◆ Did Robinson sell company secrets to our competitors?

Questions of Evaluation

In the stock issues analysis of a question of evaluation there are three headings: issues of criteria, issues of data, and issues of quality. Notice that the only difference in headings as compared with questions of fact is the first, issues of criteria.

The issue of criteria is applied to the evaluative word in the question. Consider the question, "Who is the best teacher on campus?" Understanding of the evaluative word "best" is not complete until some criteria for measuring the word's meaning is determined. In this case, a "best" teacher may be one who is knowledgeable, enthusiastic, concerned for students, fair in grading, and so forth. So, before any evaluation can take place, the criteria must be made clear.

The second issue, data, is considered much the same way as with questions of fact. If you are considering "Who is the best teacher on campus?" you have to seek out the data for each nominee to show whether each meets the criteria. Thus, the application of data is affected by the criteria selected.

The third issue, quality, is treated exactly the same way as with a question of fact. There may be extenuating circumstances that must be considered regardless of the criteria or data established.

The issues to be considered to resolve a question of evaluation can be summarized as follows:

1. By what criteria can we measure the evaluative terms? *(criteria)*

2. What are the data that determine whether the criteria are met? *(data)*

3. What, if any, extenuating circumstances affect the decision? *(quality)*

To illustrate the application of this framework, let us consider a closed and an open question of evaluation and then consider a question of direct comparison.

Question of Evaluation

Closed	*Open*
Is the SAT an effective test for predicting a high school student's success in college?	What is the most effective test available for predicting a high school student's success in college?
1. What are the criteria for determining an "effective test for predicting success"? *(criteria)*	1. What are the criteria for determining an "effective test for predicting success"? *(criteria)*
2. What are the data related to the SAT as a predictor? *(data)*	2. What are the available tests? *(data)*
3. Do the data match with the criteria well enough to support the evaluation "effective"? *(data*—matching data with criteria)	3. What are the data related to each of the available tests? *(data)*
4. What circumstances, if any, affect the decision? *(quality)*	4. In which of the tests do the data match with the criteria well enough to support the evaluation "most effective"? *(data*—matching data with criteria)
	5. What circumstances, if any, affect the decision? *(quality)*

Question of Direct Comparison

Is a vocational education or a liberal arts education better for a college student?

1. What are the criteria for determining a "better education"? *(criteria)*
2. What are the facts related to each of the types of education? *(data)*
3. Which type of education has more facts in its favor? *(data*—matching facts with criteria)
4. What circumstances, if any, affect the decision? *(quality)*

EXERCISES

Write a list of appropriate questions for discussion based on a stock issues analysis of each of the following questions of evaulation:

1.
What was the best movie of the last year?

2.
Is *Newsweek* a better news magazine than *Time?*

Questions of Policy

The stock issues approach to a question of policy usually assumes that there is a problem-solution situation. Our decision is suggested by the existence of a problem situation that can be changed, remedied, or improved. Potential decisions can than be considered on the basis of whether they are able to change, remedy, or improve the situation without creating more problems than they solve. Within such an analysis are four issues that can be adapted to nearly any question of policy. The first two issues concern the nature of the problem; the last two issues concern the effects of the proposed solution.

Size and scope of a problem   Suppose a student group is formed to resolve the question "What should be done to cope with the problem of theft in college dormitories?" The question presupposes the existence of a problem with theft. But a group cannot proceed on assumption. The group's first step is to determine the size and the scope of the problem. If the group finds that there is a problem, that it is significant, and that it is not being remedied, then the group can proceed with its analysis. If, however, there is no problem, the problem is not significant, or the problem is already being treated, then the group can conclude that no recommendation for any change is necessary.

Cause Most problems are solved by removing their causes. To get a proper understanding of the nature of a problem, we must determine what causes it and what sustains it. With the question of "What should be done to cope with the problem of theft in college dormitories?" the group may discover a number of potential causes. Some of these causes may be general—that is, so broad based that they result in many effects. Economic conditions, for example, are general causes. In times of recession, unemployment, and inflation, conditions are created that contribute to theft. Other causes may be more specific. Suppose that the college dorms have open visitation. Allowing people to come in and out of the dormitories at all hours may increase the opportunity for theft. Open visitation, then, may be a specific cause. Study of any problem will reveal several potential general and specific causes.

Before a group can begin to evaluate potential solutions it has to know what issues must be dealt with. Listing of symptoms and causes of a problem provides both insight into the nature of the problem and a framework of criteria against which suggested proposals may be measured. This leads us into a discussion of the two issues related to the proposed solution itself.

Cure Sometimes proposals look good and sound good but do not really cure the problem. With the question "What should be done to cope with the problem of theft in college dormitories?" one obvious solution is to hire more police officers. The question then becomes, "Will more police reduce instances of theft?" If it can be shown that having more police available does little in lowering instances of dormitory theft, it may be argued that the solution of hiring more police would not solve the problem. If, on the other hand, it can be shown that on campuses where more police have been hired theft in dormitories has decreased, the proposed solution of hiring more police cures or solves the problems. If it can be shown that a proposed solution does not solve the problem, it should be rejected.

Cost—Time, Money, or Social Upheaval Any change in policy will create costs. Keep in mind that cost is not only measured in money; it is also measured in time, energy, and social upheaval. As the proposed solution is examined, it is necessary to determine whether the costs will outweigh the benefits. For instance, suppose it is determined that hiring more police will decrease the number of thefts in dorms. If it is discovered that five police officers must be hired to make any significant decrease in theft, it might be argued that the monetary cost of hiring that many police outweighs the potential benefits. If there is no money to hire police, the costs would outweigh the benefits even if additional police are guaranteed to lower instances of theft. Whether or not a solution cures the problem, if its costs are too great, the solution may have to be rejected.

The following is a framework for analyzing a question of policy:

1.   What is the nature of the problem? *(size and scope)*
     a. What is the size of the problem?
     b. What are its symptoms?

2.   What are the causes of the problem? *(cause)*
     a. What are the general causes?
     b. What are the specific causes?

3.   What are the proposed solutions?

4.   Which of the plans best solves the problem or provides the greatest benefits? *(cure)*

5.   Which of the plans can be implemented with the lowest costs in time, energy, money, or social upheaval? Which plan provides the best balance between cure and costs? *(cost)*

Let us consider application of this analysis to one open and one closed question of policy.

Open Question of Policy

What should be done to equalize athletic opportunities on campus among men and women?
1. Is there inequality in athletic opportunities for women and men? *(size and scope)*
   a. How much inequality exists?
   b. What are the symptoms of these inequalities?
2. What has caused the inequalities? *(cause)*
   a. What are the general causes?
   b. What are the specific causes?
3. What are potential solutions to the problems of inequality of opportunity?
4. Which solution best solves the problem? *(cure)*
5. Which solution can be implemented with the least cost? *(cost)*

Closed Question of Policy

Should the ABC company hire a public relations specialist?
1. Is there a problem with the company's public relations? *(size and scope)*
   a. What is the size of the problem?
   b. What are its symptoms?
2. What is the cause of the company's poor public relations efforts? *(cause)*
   a. What are the general causes?
   b. What are the specific causes?
3. Would hiring a public relations specialist solve the problems? *(cure)*
4. Could a public relations specialist be hired without undue costs to the company? *(cost)*

Is a question of policy always problem-solution oriented? Although most questions of policy assume that there is a problem, a question of policy can consider alternate choices. For instance, a company may decide that there is no problem with its line of goods, but it has an opportunity to purchase a small company that produces an entirely different line of goods. Earlier we said that if there is no problem, we would recommend no change. There is, however, one set of circumstances in which a policy can be considered in its own right. We call this a question of "comparative advantage." If the proposal offers significant benefits and if the costs of implementation are not significant, the proposal may be adopted on the basis of its "comparative advantage." Thus, a company may decide to purchase a smaller company producing a different line of goods solely because of the benefits to the company. In this case the entire decision is made on the basis of issues of cure (in this case benefits) and cost.

Let us look at a question of comparative advantage in outline form.

Question of Comparative Advantage

Should the ABC company purchase Apex Products?
1. There is no size and scope to the problem because there is no problem that this purchase cures. If such a purchase is made, it would have to be justified by its "comparative advantage."
2. What are the benefits to ABC in the purchase of Apex products? *(cure-benefits)*
   a. Can major benefits be identified?
   b. Are these benefits significant?
3. Would the cost of purchasing Apex Products outweigh the comparative advantages? *(cost)*

EXERCISES

Write a list of appropriate questions for discussion based on a stock issues analysis of each of the following questions of policy:

1. Should American automobile companies be required to install airbags in their new cars?

2. What should American companies do to cope with the pressure of increased foreign imports?

Regardless of the type of question being considered, groups should acquire the habit of writing the key subquestions of the framework of analysis. After the group has discussed each of the subquestions, someone should record the group's decision on that subquestion. If possible, the group should have a written sketch of the key material used in support of each decision. Thus when the group finishes its deliberations, it will have an outline of questions, decisions, and support that can be submitted to the parent group or that can provide the basis for a written recommendation from the committee. We will consider means of obtaining a written record in Chapter 9, ''Drawing Conclusions in Groups.''

Summary

Analysis is the subdividing of a question. It is a cognitive process that requires the decision-maker to think about procedure.

Analysis of a question depends on the identification of the issues that are relevant to that question. An issue is a vital question that must be considered if the decision is to be justified. A person or a group can uncover the key issues by making a background analysis or a stock issues analysis.

A background analysis examines the historical context of the question and determines the immediate causes for considering the topic.

A stock analysis provides a framework based on a universal set of subquestions that can be applied to each type of question. Stock issues for questions of fact and evaluation grow from consideration of definition or criteria, consideration of data, and consideration of quality.

The framework of a stock issues analysis of a question of fact includes: (1) definitions of key terms, (2) relevant data that satisfy the definition or determine classifications, and (3) extenuating circumstances. The framework of a stock issues analysis of a question of evaluation includes: (1) criteria by which each evaluative term is measured, (2) data that determine whether criteria are met, and (3) extenuating circumstances.

Stock issues of a question of policy grow from the existence and scope of a problem, the causes of the problem, the costs of any change in policy, and the consequences of the cure.

The framework of a stock issues analysis of a question of policy includes: (1) the nature of the problem, (2) the causes of the problem (3) determination of whether the proposed solution solves the problem and (4) determination of whether the solution can be implemented without undue cost.

6

RESEARCHING THE QUESTION

Once you have agreed to be a part of a decision-making group, you have a responsibility to work. Many people think of the group experience as one where people "bat around ideas." But your responsibility involves getting ready for as well as participating in the group discussion. So, instead of the "Well, here I am, what do we do now?" attitude, you need to take an active part in preparing. You should never go into a group decision-making session unless you have done your homework. In this chapter we will look at sources of information, kinds of information, recording of information, use of information and testing of information.

Sources of Information

There are several sources of information you can tap to help you get ready for group decision making.

Circulated Information

In some decision-making groups you will not be required to gather information—it will be done for you. Another group or resource person may be responsible for accumulating information and circulating it to group members. But the whole idea of circulating information is short-circuited if you don't take the time to read the information before the group meeting. In a group, it is easy to leave the work to the other guy. Adopt the attitude that you *are* the other guy! *Read circulated information carefully.*

Personal Experience

There is a chance that the question being discussed is one that you have thought about or worked with before. For instance, if your group is considering a plan for distributing available parking space so that it is equally fair to administrators, faculty, and students, your parking experience may be useful to the group. But, your experience should, whenever possible, be validated. Personal experience can be a part of your preparation, but it is seldom enough for your total preparation.

Library Sources

For many questions, you will need solid, documented materials. Suppose you are considering changing college requirements. What are the requirements at other colleges and universities? Your library carries catalogues of other schools that you can check. Or suppose you are considering instituting a course on television criticism. Your library carries various magazines and journals that will have articles related to the issue. For any question, you may need to do library research to be prepared.

Let us take a look at library sources that are considered basic research tools. These should be considered general knowledge materials for any college student.

Card Catalog   The card catalog indexes all library materials by author, title, and subject. The principal use of the card catalog is to locate the best books related to your question.

Periodicals and Magazines   Periodicals are publications that appear at fixed intervals: weekly, biweekly, monthly, quarterly, or yearly. The information in weekly, biweekly, and monthly magazines is more current than information in books. Of course, some magazines are more accurate, more complete, and more useful than others. Since you must know where and how to find articles before you can evaluate them, you should know and use three indexes: the *Readers' Guide to Periodical Literature,* the *Education Index,* and the *Index to Behavioral Sciences and Humanities.*

The *Readers' Guide to Periodical Literature* indexes approximately 150 popular magazines and journals, and is by far the most valuable source for questions of current interest.

If your question is related to the field of education, including subjects such as school administration, adult education, film strips, intelligence, morale, tests and scales, Project Head Start, or ungraded schools, *Education Index,* a cumulative subject index to a selected list of about 150 educational periodicals, proceedings, and yearbooks, will lead you to the available sources.

In contrast to the *Readers' Guide,* which lists articles in popular journals, the *Index to Behavioral Sciences and Humanities* lists articles from about 150 scholarly journals such as *American Journal of Sociology, Economist, Modern Language Quarterly,* and *Philosophical Review.*

Encyclopedias   Encyclopedias give an excellent overview of many subjects and offer valuable bibliographies, but because the articles could not possibly cover every topic completely, relatively few are detailed. In addition, an encyclopedia is seldom of value for the changing facts and details needed for contemporary problems because its information becomes dated. Most libraries have recent editions of *Encyclopaedia Britannica, Encyclopedia Americana,* or *World Book Encyclopedia.*

Biographical Sources   When you need biographical details, from thumbnail sketches to complete essays, you can turn to one of the many biographical sources available. In addition to full-length books and encyclopedia entries, you should explore books such as *Who's Who* and *Who's Who in America* (short sketches of British subjects and American citizens, respectively) or *Dictionary of National Biography* and *Dictionary of American Biography* (complete essays about prominent British subjects and American citizens, respectively).

Statistical Sources   When you need facts, details, or statistics about population, records, continents, heads of state, weather, or similar subjects, you should refer to one of the many single-volume sources that report such data. Three of the most noteworthy sources in this category are *World Almanac and Book of Facts* (1868 to date), *Statistical Abstract of the United States* (1878 to date), and *Statesman's Yearbook: Statistical and Historical Annual of the States of the World* (1867 to date).

Newspapers   Despite the relatively poor quality of reporting in many of our daily newspapers, newspaper articles should not be overlooked as sources of facts and interpretations of contemporary problems. Your library probably holds both an index of the nearest major daily and the *New York Times Index*.

Library holdings will vary, your library may well have other bibliographies, indexes, and special resources available. Your reference librarian can help you to familiarize yourself with additional materials.

Public Opinion

For some questions, a survey of public opinion may be the most appropriate way of collecting information. In considering a decision about the distribution of available parking space, you may be able to take advantage of the experience and opinions of people who currently use the parking space. What do they think of the current system? What would they like to see done? Prepare a few well-worded questions, and go the parking lots and ask your questions. If a personal survey is not practicable, put your survey questionnaire under the windshield wiper of every car. Ask each driver to answer the questions and to leave the results at the entry gate or to drop them in the campus mail. You need data to work with, and taking a survey is a good way of getting information. You will want to make sure that you have polled a large enough group and that you have sampled different segments of the larger group before you attempt to draw any significant conclusions from your poll.

As time goes on, you may find yourself gaining considerable experience and expertise in research design and statistical methods. At such a time, you may find that survey data collection is the most important means of collecting information. Many agencies pay consultants well to conduct statistical surveys and provide decision-making groups with the data.

Interviews

An effective, but often overlooked, means of preparation is the personal interview. One interview with the right person may be all that is needed. On the other hand, you may have to interview several people to get all the information you need. Because interviewing is likely to be the method of information gathering you know the least about, let's look at three of the most important steps of good interviewing: selecting the best person, determining a procedure, and conducting the interview.

Selecting the Best Person   Either on campus or in the larger community, there are persons who have expertise in the problem areas you want to research. Your first step should be to find out who they are so you can arrange to talk with them. Suppose you are interested in the selection and preparation of your school cafeteria's food. Whom should you interview? Perhaps one of the employees can tell you who is in charge of the dining hall. Perhaps you need to call a particular campus agency. After you have made a list of names, an appointment with one or more persons on the list. Making an appointment is very important—you cannot just walk into an office and expect the prospective interviewee to drop everything on the spur of the moment. You are not going to get much valuable information if the person is not willing to cooperate with you. To get an appointment you must know (1) why you need to interview this particular person and (2) what information you hope to get from the interview.

Before conducting the interview, you should do some research on the person you will be interviewing. If you are going to interview the dietitian who makes out menus and orders the food, you should know something about the job of dietitian and something about the problems involved in ordering and preparing institutional food. Not only will evidence of preliminary research encourage the person to talk more openly with you (few people will respect or talk in detail with someone who obviously knows nothing about them or the subject), but familiarity with material will enable you to frame more penetrating questions. If for some reason you are unable to get any preliminary information, at least approach the interviewee with a degree of enthusiasm and apparent interest in his or her job.

In addition, you should be forthright in your reasons for seeking the interview. Whether you are interviewing the person as part of a class project or are writing a newspaper article on campus food, make your purpose clear.

Determining a Procedure   Good interviewing results from careful planning. The plan includes an overall method and preparation of specific questions. Because questioning is the most important tool of a good interviewer, let us look at the kinds of questions you need to prepare. Questions may be open or closed, primary or secondary, neutral or leading.

1.   Open and closed questions. Open questions are broad-based. They range from those having no restrictions, such as "Tell me about cave exploring," to those that give specific directions, such as "Tell me about how you prepare yourself to explore a new cave." Why do interviewers use open questions? The open question encourages the responding person to talk, allowing the interviewer maximum opportunity to listen and to observe. Using the open question, the interviewer finds out about the interviewee's feelings, attitudes, values, and so forth in relation to the subject area. Open questions take more time, and the interviewer can lose direction if he or she is not careful.

Closed questions range from those that require only yes or no answers ("Have you ever explored any caves that are uncharted?") to those that require only a few words ("How many caves have you explored this year?" or "What kinds of situations give a cave explorer the most problems?"). With the closed question, the interviewer can control the interview; moreover, he or she can collect much information in a short time. On the other hand, the closed question seldom enables the interviewer to learn why a person gives a certain response. Neither is the closed question likely to yield much voluntary information.

Which type of question is superior for the interviewer? The answer depends on what kinds of material you are seeking and on how much time you have for the interview. An opinion-poll interviewer who wants specific responses to specific questions will rely mostly or entirely on closed questions. A person who is primarily interested in the thoughts and feelings of another person might ask only open questions. In an information-gathering interview for a speech, you will want enough closed questions to get the specifics you need and enough open questions to allow for anecdotes, illustrations, and personal views.

2.   Primary and secondary questions. Primary questions introduce topics, and secondary questions follow up on the answers to primary questions. Primary questions are determined before the interview. Framing good secondary questions requires the interviewer to pay close attention to what is happening. Both primary and secondary questions may have open or closed phrasing.

Using secondary questions motivates the respondent to enlarge on an answer that appears inadequate. Follow-ups are necessary because the respondent may purposely be evasive, incomplete, or vague, or because the interviewee may not really understand how much detail you are looking for.

As an interviewer, you must tailor your questions to the circumstances. If you want to encourage the respondent to continue, you should use such questions as ''And then?'' ''Is there more?'' and ''What happened next?'' If you want to probe more deeply into an area, you should use such follow-up questions as ''What do you mean by 'frequently'?'' ''What were you thinking at the time?'' and ''Can you give me some examples?'' If you want to plumb the feelings of the respondent, you might ask such secondary questions as ''How did it feel to be stuck underground?'' ''Were you worried when you didn't find her?'' and ''Did you feel any resentment when you weren't selected?''

Your effectiveness with follow-up questions may depend on your skill in asking them. Because probing questions can alienate the interviewer (especially when the questions are perceived as threatening), in-depth probes work best after you have gained the confidence of the respondent and when you ask such questions within the atmosphere of a positive interpersonal climate.

3.   Neutral and leading questions. Neutral questions are those in which the respondent is free to give an answer without direction. Leading questions are those in which the interviewer suggests the answer that is expected or desired. A neutral question would be ''How do you like working on a team with a famous explorer?'' A leading question would be ''Being on a team with a famous explorer is intimidating, isn't it?'' The neutral question leaves it to the respondent to determine how to answer. With a leading question, the person feels some pressure to answer in a particular way. Because leading questions are frequently used to control the attitude or behavior of the respondent, the leading question is usually inappropriate for information-getting interviews.

To start the interview, you should thank the person for taking time to talk with you. Try to develop good rapport with your respondent from the start. Ask questions that can be answered easily and that will show your respect for the person you are interviewing. For instance, in an interview with the head dietitian, you might start with a question such as ''How did you get interested in nutrition?'' or ''I imagine planning menus can be a very challenging job in these times of high food costs—is that so?'' After the person nods or says yes, you can ask about the biggest challenges he or she faces. The goal is to get the interviewee to feel at ease and to talk freely. Since the most important consideration of this initial stage is to create a positive communication climate, keep the questions easy to answer, nonthreatening, and encouraging.

The body of the interview includes the major questions you have prepared. Plan to group questions so that the easy-to-answer questions come first and the hard-hitting questions that require careful thinking come later. For instance, the question "What do you do to answer student complaints?" should be near the end of the interview. You may not ask all the questions you planned to ask, but don't end the interview until you have gotten all the important information you intended to get. When you finish asking your questions, thank the person again for taking time to talk with you.

The following example gives a method of setting up a schedule of interview questions. If you were planning to interview the dietitian, you might prepare the following questions:

I. Background
   A. What background and training do you need for the job?
   B. How did you get interested in nutrition?
   C. Have you worked as a dietitian for long?
   D. Have you held any other food-related positions?

II. Responsibilities
   A. What are the responsibilities of your job besides meal planning?
   B. How far in advance are meals planned?
   C. What factors are taken into account when you are planning the meals for a given period?
   D. Do you have a free hand or are there constraints placed on you?

III. Procedures
   A. Is there a specific number of times you put a given item on the menu?
   B. Do you take individual differences into account?
   C. How do you determine whether or not you will give choices for the entree?
   D. What do you do to answer student complaints?
   E. Can a student get a comparable meal at a good cafeteria for the same money? Explain.

Conducting the Interview   The best plan in the world will not result in a good interview unless you practice good interpersonal communication skills in conducting the interview. Let us focus on a few of the particularly important interpersonal elements of good interviewing. More than anything else, you should be courteous during the interview. Listen carefully—your job is not to debate or to give your opinion but to get information from a person who has it. Whether you like the person or not or whether you agree with the person or not, you must respect his or her opinions—after all, you are the one who asked for the interview.

Put into practice your best listening skills. If the person has given a rather long answer to a question, you should paraphrase what has been said to make sure your interpretation is correct. Keep the interview moving. You do not want to rush the person, yet he or she is probably busy with a full schedule of activities. It is a good idea to ask for a certain amount of time when you first make the appointment. Sometimes the interviewee will want to extend the time. Ordinarily, however, when the time is up, you should call attention to the fact and be prepared to conclude.

Last, but certainly not least, you should be very much aware of the nonverbal impression you make. Consider your clothes—you want to be dressed appropriately for the occasion. Since you are taking the person's time, show an interest in the person and in what he or she has to say. How you look and act may well determine whether the person will cooperate and give you the kind of interview you want.

After you finish the interview, you should review it carefully. If you took notes, it is important to write out complete answers while information is still fresh in your mind. You may also find it necessary to check out the facts you have been given. If what the person has told you differs from material you have from other sources, double check the accuracy of the interview information.

EXERCISES

1. ◆ Divide the class into four groups. Each group should select a topic question from the following list and consider a strategy for gathering information from each of four sources: (1) personal experience, (2) written sources, (3) surveys, (4) interviews.
a. What should be done to reduce crime in the community?
b. What should be done to meet the needs of students who commute?
c. Should college requirements be revised?
d. What is the extent of drug abuse on campus?

2. ◆ You want to get information on the question of crime in the community by conducting an interview.
a. Who would be the best person to interview?
b. Devise an interview schedule for a thirty-minute interview with this person. Make sure that you include at least six major questions. Be able to justify the order of the questions.

Kinds of Information

We have talked about *where* to look for material. Let us now consider *what* to look for. You need to look for the raw material from which you will shape contributions to your group. Any information will be useful, but examples, illustrations, statistics, quotations, definitions, visual aids, and comparisons are particularly helpful.

Examples and Illustrations

"Give me an example" is a common response of group members after a point is made. An *example* is a representative sample of a generalization or an assertion. An *illustration* is a detailed example. You will draw conclusions from your experiences and observations, and you will present your conclusions (generalizations) to your group. Other group members may not have had the benefit of your experiences, and they will not be impressed by the assertions or generalizations alone. Examples help to test assertions and generalizations and to illustrate them for others. Examples make your contributions easier to comprehend or more persuasive.

The examples you find will be of three kinds: *real* examples, which indicate actual occurrences; *fictitious* examples, which allude to instances that are or have been made up to explain the point; and *hypothetical* examples, which suggest what would happen in certain circumstances.

A real example: Automobile companies are making major efforts to increase gasoline mileage, even in the largest models. Full-size cars are as much as three feet shorter than 1977 models; weight has been reduced by as much as 1,000 pounds or more; engine horsepower has been lowered considerably.

A fictitious example: Just because a person is slow does not mean that the person should be considered a loser. Remember the story of the tortoise and the hare: the tortoise, who was much slower, still won the race.

A hypothetical example: Dogs do poorly on simple intelligence tests. If a ten-foot section of fence were put between a dog and a bone, he would try to paw through the fence rather than go the five feet or so it would take to get around the fence.

Statistics

Statistics are numerical facts. Statements such as "Only six of every ten voted in the last election" or "The cost of living rose eight-tenths of 1 percent" enable you to pack a great deal of information into short comments. When statistics are well used, they can be most impressive; when they are poorly used, they may be deceiving. You wouldn't want the group to arrive at a poor decision based on unsound statistics. Statistics seem to have a bewitching force. Most of us seem conditioned to believe that evidence cast in statistical form carries real weight.

Your first and most important concern should be the accuracy of the statistics you find. Taking statistics from only the most reliable sources and double-checking them against other sources will help you avoid a great deal of difficulty. In addition, you must be aware of the dates of the statistics. Times change; what was true five, or even two, years ago may be significantly different today. For instance, in 1971 only 12 out of the 435 members of Congress were women. If your question called for data about the number of women in Congress, you would want current statistics.

After you are satisfied that you have found recent, reputable statistics, be careful how you use them. Statistics are most meaningful when they are used for comparative purposes. To say that industry offered the nation's supermarkets about 5,200 products this year does not mean much unless it is known how many products are already on the shelves.

In making comparisons, you should make sure that you do not present a misleading picture. For instance, if you say that during the past six months Company A doubled its sales while its nearest competitor, Company B, improved by only 40 percent, the implication would be misleading if you did not indicate the number of sales. Company B could have had more sales even though its improvement was only 40 percent.

Although statistics may be an excellent way of supporting material, be careful of using them too much. A few well-used statistics are far better than a barrage of numbers. Even a group that wants and needs information can be overwhelmed.

In your use of statistics and in the evaluation of their use by other group members, you should beware of at least three situations. First, beware of statistics that are impossible to verify. If you are like me, you have read countless startling statements such as "15 million mosquitoes are hatched each day in the Canadian province of Ontario." Now don't quote this one—I made it up; but it is no more unlikely than many other examples I have seen. We have no way of verifying such statistics. Does anyone count the number of mosquitoes hatched? Statistics of this kind are startling and make for interesting conversation, but as support for decision making they must be suspect.

Second, beware of statistics that are used alone. By themselves, statistics do not really mean much. "Last season the Cincinnati Reds drew slightly more than 2 million fans to their seventy home games." Although this sounds like (and is) a lot of people, it does not tell much about the club's attendance. Is this figure high or low? Was attendance up or down? How does this compare to attendance figures of other clubs? Statistics of this kind are not meaningful until they are compared with other data.

Third, beware of statistics used with an unknown comparative base. Comparisons between and among statistics do not mean much if the comparative base is not given. Consider the following statement: "While the Zolon economic growth rate was dawdling along at 3 percent last year, Allon was growing at a healthy 8 percent." This statement implies that Allon is doing much better than Zolon. However, if Zolon's economic base were larger, its 3 percent increase could be much better than Allon's 8 percent. We cannot know unless we understand the entire economic base.

Quotations

You are likely to find that some, if not a great deal, of the information you want to submit to the group will be direct quotation. If you find that a writer's explanation or opinion is valuable either for the quality of the information or for the effective way it is phrased, you may want to present it precisely as stated. Under some circumstances you may be able to bring the work with you and quote directly. Often, however, you will want only the information itself. If that is the case, record the material carefully, making sure that your quotation is accurate.

You must not, however, read great amounts of material during the discussion. Long quotations are boring to listen to and difficult to digest. It is much better to condense long passages into short statements. Quote only those ideas that are especially well stated or especially important.

Definitions

Definitions provide meanings for words we use. Our entire language is built on the assumption that we, as a culture, share common meanings of words. Yet most of us can define only a fraction of the words in the English language, and few of us are likely to define even fairly common words in the same way. Still, with every kind of discussion question a definition may be the key to a good decision. As I have noted, the first issue in questions of fact and evaluation has to do with definition. I recommend looking for definitions of key words in your reading. The group will have to come to agreement on meanings before much progress can be made. Written definitions are likely to be carefully thought out, and as a result, quite useful.

Visual Aids

Nearly every type of information we have discussed can be represented to a group by using visual aids. Sets of figures or a particular bit of information may be so important to the decision-making process that it might be well worth while to prepare visual aids. By using a sketch, a chart, a graph, or a map, you might be able to communicate a point that you couldn't otherwise make clear.

Comparisons

I have mentioned several times the value of comparing statistics, examples, and other types of information. Let us consider the options you have available.

Comparison involves showing the similarities or differences between two entities. Comparisons may be figurative or literal. A *figurative comparison* expresses something symbolically. For example, we may speak of a person who is "slow as a turtle," meaning that he or she moves extremely slowly in comparison to other persons. A *literal comparison* is an actual comparison. We may say that a retail store is the same size as Macy's.

Comparisons may be made using metaphors or similes. A *metaphor* is a figure of speech in which a word or phrase that literally denotes one kind of object or idea is used in place of another. "Product liability is a growing world fire that could consume industry" is a metaphor. A *simile* is a figure of speech in which a thing or idea is likened to another. The words *like, as,* and *than* are used in similes. "He walks like an elephant" and "His grip is like a vise" are both similes.

Occasionally, a comparison is cast as a *contrast* and focuses on differences rather than similarities. "Unlike last year when we did mostly period drama, this year we are producing mostly comedies and musicals," is a contrast. As you do your research, try to find comparisons that will help you express your ideas more clearly. When you cannot find a comparison, create one for use in the discussion.

Recording of Information

In your research (including personal observation, interviewing, and written sources), you may find a variety of examples, illustrations, quotations, statistics, and comparisons that you want access to for discussion. How should you record these materials so that they will be of greatest value? You will be able to use only a fraction of the material you find, and you can never be sure of the order in which you will use the materials. Therefore, you need a method of recording that will allow you to select, order, and use materials to best meet your needs.

The *notecard method* is probably the best. As you find materials, record each item separately on a 3″ × 5″ or 4″ × 6″ cards. It may seem easier to record materials from one source on a single sheet of paper or on a large card, but sorting and arranging material is much easier when each item is recorded on a separate card. In addition to recording each item separately, you should indicate the name of the source, the name of the author, and the page number from which the item was taken. You will not necessarily need this material, but if you decide to quote directly or to reexamine a point, you will know the source. Figure 6-1 illustrates a useful notecard form.

Topic: Dealing with Federal Fraud

"So far, Reagan auditors have challenged
governmental transactions totaling $142 million;
they have recovered $99 million and have filed
appeals to collect the remainder. Criminal
charges 'in those cases have resulted in 400
convicions."

"The Crackdown on Federal Fraud," Newsweek,
September 7, 1981, p. 17.

Figure 6-1. The notecard method for recording information.

As you gather the sources that will be included in your research, you may find that you have discovered more material than you can possibly read. In order to locate and record the best material, you should develop a system of evaluation that will enable you to review the most information in the shortest period of time. Most students find that with a little practice they can increase their efficiency by skip reading. If you are appraising a magazine article, spend a minute or two finding out what it covers. Does it present information on the phase of the topic you are exploring? Does it contain any documented statistics, examples, or quotable opinions? Is the author qualified to draw meaningful conclusions? If you are appraising a book, read the table of contents carefully, look at the index, and skip-read pertinent chapters. Ask the same questions as you would for appraising a magazine article. During the skip-reading period, decide which sources should be read in full, which should be read in part, and which should be abandoned. Such evaluation will save you from reading useless material.

Using Facts as Evidence

The facts and opinions you use to prove points are called *evidence*. Let us consider the major categories of evidence and examine the comparative value of each.

Primary and Secondary Evidence

Primary evidence is material in its original state. Diaries or letters are primary evidence of a person's thoughts. The report of a research study in a scientific journal is primary evidence of that study's findings. Department of Labor statistics about employment and unemployment are primary evidence of those statistics.

Secondary evidence comes from a source that refers to or uses primary evidence. If in a history book the author discusses a person's opinions taken from his or her letters and diaries, the book is secondary evidence. A textbook that explains the findings of a communication researcher is secondary evidence of those findings. *Time* magazine's account of employment statistics based on Department of Labor statistics is secondary evidence of those statistics.

Primary evidence is preferable to secondary evidence because it is original. Secondary evidence is second hand and is at least once removed from primary evidence. Although secondary evidence may be and often is accurate, its accuracy should be questioned. As evidence goes from source to source it is likely to be distilled, shortened, diluted, or sometimes distorted. As a result, it is unlikely that evidence two or three times removed will be as accurate as primary evidence.

When possible, use primary sources of evidence. When your material comes from secondary sources, you may need to trace its primary sources in order to verify its accuracy.

Written or Oral Evidence

Written evidence is any evidence that comes from written sources such as reports, books, magazines or letters. Oral evidence is taken from a person's conversation, interviews, or speech. Oral evidence is further subdivided into first-hand testimony and hearsay. *First-hand testimony* of observation is considered solid enough to be admissible as evidence in courts of law—but only when it is taken under oath. A person may only report what he or she has seen directly. But oral evidence may also be hearsay. *Hearsay evidence* is second-hand evidence. When a person reports, ''I heard Tom tell about what he saw at the camp,'' such evidence is hearsay and is not admissible in court. The argument against using such testimony as evidence is that first-hand testimony can be subject to cross-examination, but hearsay evidence may not. If you are reporting what you have seen, another person can question you in order to determine the quality of your observation. When you are reporting hearsay, the original source is not present and cannot be questioned.

Written evidence is preferable to oral evidence because it is easier to verify. Even though first-hand testimony is admissible in courts of law as evidence, studies have shown that people rarely report even first-hand observations accurately. If your evidence is oral, you must make every effort to verify it before using it as the basis for decision making.

Expert or Lay Evidence

Expert evidence comes from a source recognized as an authority in the field. *Lay evidence* comes from a person whose major field of expertise lies elsewhere.

Expert evidence is preferable to lay evidence. Whether the evidence is fact or opinion, we are likely to consider the credibility of the source in determining its value. Thus, a historian is more likely to be believed than a mathematician on the subject of current U.S. foreign policy. Likewise, a space biologist's opinion about the presence of life on other planets will be given more credence than an auto mechanic's opinion.

Do not discount all lay evidence, however. There are times when lay opinion is quite valuable. Some people have knowledge of several subject areas, and their comments are worthy of consideration.

Direct Evidence or Circumstantial Evidence

Direct evidence bears a direct relationship to what is being proved. *Circumstantial evidence* proves something indirectly by proving other events or circumstances that provide a basis for reasonable conclusions. For instance, in a court of law, motive, opportunity, and access to the weapon are circumstantial evidence of guilt. Eye-witness testimony is direct evidence.

Direct evidence is preferable to circumstantial evidence, but there are times when circumstantial evidence is the only evidence available. As many court cases show, circumstantial evidence can make a difference in the outcome of a trial.

EXERCISES

1. ♦ Label each of the following statements of evidence with: (P) primary; (S) secondary; (W) written; (O) oral; (E) expert; (L) lay; (D) direct; and (C) circumstantial. Each statement will have more than one label.

2. ♦ Indicate which pair of statements should be given more weight in your group discussion. Why?

_____ In an article appearing in the June 16, 1981 **Time** magazine, it was reported . . .

_____ In a conversation I overheard in the student union dining hall, Mark said . . .

_____ Henry Steele Commager, the noted historian, wrote that in their letters home, soldiers often complained about food.

_____ By scanning the unedited collection of soldier's letters that was published recently, we can see how often soldiers wrote about their complaints with food.

Testing of Information

Your group is going to want to make decisions on the basis of sound evidence. To assure yourself of the quality of the information presented, apply the following major tests to determine quantity, recency, documentation, objectivity, and reliability of the source.

Quantity of Evidence

Is there enough evidence to support the point? Although it is sometimes difficult to determine how much is enough, a single item of evidence is rarely enough to provide conclusive proof. For most subjects, you will want to see a quantity of evidence that supports the same conclusion. The fewer the items of evidence that are used to prove a point, the better that evidence will have to be. For example, a temperature of 102° is enough evidence to show that a person is sick, since fever is a medically accepted standard for determining sickness. A runny nose, on the other hand, is not enough evidence to prove that a person has an allergy. More evidence would be needed to substantiate such a claim.

A reasonable amount of evidence includes material for each subpoint of your group's outline. Although comprehensive research on any subject could take a team of researchers weeks or more, your group research should be comprehensive ''within reason.'' ''Within reason'' might be defined as using at least four or more sources of information and having several bits of evidence in support of each point you are considering.

Recency of Evidence

Is the evidence recent? In our age, as never before, products, ideas, and other data quickly become obsolete. Be alert to when the particular data were true and when they were stated to be true. Five-year-old data may not be true today. In scientific or technological circles, two-year-old data may be obsolete. You may find an article in last month's *Time* that is using five-year-old data, so recency of a secondary source is not necessarily evidence of recency of data.

Documentation of Evidence

Is the evidence verifiable? Although some evidence is common knowledge, you must be able to document it. Your best bet is to take nothing for granted.

It is much better to have too much verification for evidence than too little. Evidence is verified by (1) showing where the evidence comes from and (2) indicating that the source is trustworthy. For instance, if Connie says that she heard that the new department head has been selected, the evidence is hearsay and difficult to verify. On the other hand, if Connie reports that she has received a letter from the dean announcing the appointment of a new department head, her testimony is better. Producing the letter and reading from it would provide the best verification for her statement.

Objectivity of Evidence

Is the source biased? Sometimes even a good source has to be discounted because of an apparent bias. If Paul recommends his brother for a job, Paul's recommendation may be considered biased. Everyone has a blind spot or a bias. If we discover that the evidence presented is the result of a person's blind spot, we may want to discount the value of that evidence.

The best evidence is that admitted even by those you expect to be biased on the other side of the question. If an opponent of an idea admits the validity of evidence, you can usually trust in its soundness.

Reliability of Source

Is the source of the evidence reliable and competent? Especially if the evidence is oral, you must ask such questions as "Did the source observe directly?" "Is the source capable of reporting objectively?" "Is the source respectable?" and "Is the source usually worthy of belief?"

Any source that you read will be a combination of fact and opinion. A fact is verifiable; an opinion is an expressed view. That apples have seeds is a fact; that apples taste good is an opinion. Some opinions are related to, based on, or extended from facts—some are not. Before you build your case, you need to test the accuracy of your facts and the objectivity of your opinions.

Determining the accuracy of every item in a source can be long and tedious, and perhaps even an impossible, job. In most cases accuracy can be reasonably assured by checking the fact against the original source. If your source states that, according to the most recent Department of Labor statistics, unemployment went down 0.2 percent in December, check the most recent Department of Labor statistics. If your history book footnotes the source of an important quotation, check the original source. Although checking sources in this way may appear to be an unnecessary task, you will be surprised at the number of errors that occur in using data from other sources.

If the original or primary source is not available, check the fact against the facts in another source on the subject. Two or more sources may on occasion get their "facts" from the same faulty source, but when two or more sources state the same fact or similar facts, the chances of accuracy are considerably increased.

Facts by themselves are not nearly as important as the conclusions drawn from them. Since conclusions are usually opinions, they have to be weighed carefully before they can be accepted. Researchers study a variety of sources to see what they say about the same facts; then they draw their own conclusions from the facts. Your conclusion may duplicate one source, may draw from several sources, or may differ from the sources. Only after you have examined many sources are you in a position to make the kind of value judgment that a thinking decision maker needs to make. In your research, you may be surprised at how many times two sources will appear to contradict each other on the interpretation of a set of facts. Whether the issue is the causes of violence, the effects of birth-control pills on women, or the importance of free trade to a nation's economic position, what the source says may depend on the biases of the author, the availability or selection of material, or the care taken in evaluating the data. Thus, decision makers must be sure that they are not communicating a distorted, biased, or hastily stated opinion as fact.

Summary

Quality decisions result largely from high-quality information.

Information for your decision making may come from a variety of sources. If material is circulated, you should read it carefully *before* a group meeting. If you are expected to do research, and this is most likely to be the case, begin by surveying your own personal information. For some topics, library sources will provide the greatest amount of information. You may find that time spent surveying public opinion can also get you vital information. And certainly you should learn the value of the interview.

Regardless of the source of the material, there are certain kinds of information that will prove especially valuable, including examples and illustrations, statistics, quotations, visual aids, and comparisons.

To handle the large amount of information you will process, you need a note-taking method. By putting information on note cards you will find it much easier to organize the material for use in group discussion.

In your group, you will use information as evidence. Evidence is material used to prove points. Primary evidence, material in its original state, is better than secondary evidence, material that is taken second-hand. Written evidence is preferable to oral evidence. Expert evidence is preferable to lay evidence, and direct evidence is preferable to circumstantial evidence.

Ultimately, the evidence you use must be tested. You test evidence on the basis of quantity presented, recency, quality of documentation, objectivity, and reliability of the source.

7

DISCUSSING THE QUESTION

Taking part in group decision making requires talking. Good preparation is the starting point for productive participation, but how you talk, when you talk, and why you talk determine your effectiveness in the group.

This chapter begins by assuming that you are willing to participate. The adage "Two heads are better than one" is only true when the two heads are willing to share ideas. Not only does everyone have the right to talk, but everyone must be willing to exercise that right.

Some discussions are more productive than others. To be most effective in your group, you must master a number of skills that relate to the task and maintenance functions that were mentioned in Chapter 3. In this chapter we will consider three basic skills that seem most important to productive participation: sharing information, responding to information, and organizing information.[1]

Sharing Information

As was mentioned earlier, sharing information involves about 50 percent of a group's time. Good information and well-considered opinions provide the group with the material necessary to make good decisions. Some of the key skills of sharing information are maintaining objectivity, stating information provisionally, dating information, indexing generalizations, and citing sources.

Maintaining Objectivity

Objectivity is essential in decision making, yet as you think about research, and discuss the major issues of a question, you may find yourself advocating a particular idea, plan, or procedure. Advocacy begets ego involvement, and once you become ego involved in your material, you lose your objectivity. In debate, advocates of opposite sides of a question present their arguments in an effort to convince a judge or audience of the merits of their particular side. Group communication, however, involves presenting all sides of the question without bias. Although few people can remain objective at all times (some

---

[1]For a more complete analysis of these and other important interpersonal skills, see Rudolph F. Verderber and Kathleen S. Verderber, *Inter-Act: Using Interpersonal Communication Skills,* 2nd ed. (Belmont, Calif: Wadsworth, 1979).

scholars would argue that objectivity is itself an illusion), there are two skills that you can use to foster objectivity.

First, report data but do not associate yourself with them. If, for instance, you report that preschool children watch more than 25 hours of television each week, do not feel that because you presented the information you must defend it. The following is an example of objective reporting: "According to the May 6, 1980 issue of *Newsweek,* children under age five watch an average of 25 hours of television a week. If this information is correct, children's viewing exceeds the average for adult viewing. *Does anyone else have data to support* Newsweek's *statistic?"* The italicized sentence tells the group that you are seeking discussion of the information and that whether or not it is supported, you have no personal ties with it.

Second, try to find material supporting differing views on each of the key issues of the question. Although nothing is wrong with forming tentative opinions based on the material you've researched, you should present material you have found regardless of whether it supports or opposes your tentative position. After all material is presented, you may tell why you think one position is stronger than another. But conclusions should not be drawn until all the available material is pooled. If the group ultimately arrives at a conclusion that opposes your original tentative position, you are not put on the defensive. By being objective, you may find that during the discussion your views will change many times. Remember, if the best answer to the topic question could be found without discussion, no discussion would be necessary.

Stating Information Provisionally

You can also improve your group communication by stating information provisionally. *Provisional statements* are conditional and avoid absolute certainty or dogmatism. As a communicator you should try to phrase information so that it will not create or add to a defensive communication climate or cause unnecessary conflict. Provisional statements will facilitate an open climate of communication, but dogmatic statements will create defensiveness.

Consider the following dogmatic statements: Sales were down 10 percent last year—the first time in the history of the company that sales dropped so much in a year. Standardized tests show relative ability. This is no time to modernize the facility. All three statements assert the "truth." Although the first statement is a matter of record (it can be validated by looking at a record of the company's history), as stated it is *not* necessarily true. The other two statements are matters of opinion—they are inferences drawn from facts, but again, not necessarily true. All three statements are phrased in a way that cannot be refuted and as such will cause defensiveness.

Consider the following provisional statements: Sales were down 10 percent last year; if I remember correctly, that was the first time in the history of the company that sales dropped so much in one year. I've been taught that standardized tests show relative ability. In my opinion, this is no time to modernize. What are the differences? Why are the provisional statements more likely to result in better group communication? First, the tentativeness of the phrasing will result in a less certain tone of voice. Second, it is clear that the speaker realizes he or she may be wrong. "The first time in the history of the company that sales dropped so much in a year" says "I'm telling you what's right." "If I remember correctly . . ." says that the speaker thinks he or she is right, but there is some chance for a mistake. Recognizing the possibility of error makes it all right for the other person to offer his or her opinion without feeling defensive.

Provisional statements allow different opinions. They acknowledge that data that seem to be accurate under some circumstances may not be accurate under all circumstances.

Speaking provisionally may seem unassertive, but there is a world of difference between the provisional phrasing "From what I've read I believe Apple II is the best value in home computers" and the comment "Everyone knows Apple II is the best" delivered in a superior, surly tone of voice—one that is very likely to arouse hostility.

Dating Information

Dating means providing a specific time referent to indicate when a given fact was true. Many times when members share information they leave the impression that the information is current when in fact it may be outdated. For instance, as the group considers consequences of a new policy, Park says, "that may require several of our people and their families to move to Henderson City." Bill replies, "Good luck—they've had some real trouble with their schools." On the basis of Bill's statement, the group will be concerned with what this move might mean to employees and their families. What Park and the group don't know is that Bill is talking about a problem that Henderson City had *five years ago*. Henderson City may still have these problems, but it may not. If Bill had replied, "Five years ago they had some real trouble with their schools, but I don't know what the situation is now," the group would look at the information differently.

The fact is that nearly everything changes with time: Things and people age, grow, learn, wear out. Some changes may be imperceptible, but some changes are so great that they make the person, idea, or thing nearly unrecognizable. Thus you should always indicate, actually or mentally, the date when your view of that phenomenon was true. Consider the following phrasings:

When we were in Palm Springs *two years ago,* it was really popular with the college crowd.

Powell brings great enthusiasm to her teaching—at least she did *last quarter* in communication theory.

Four years ago Compton's was considered the best and least expensive supplier of the heavy equipment we use.

You think Mary's depressed? I'm surprised. She seemed her regular high-spirited self when I talked with her *the day before yesterday.*

Because you have no power to prevent change, you should recognize the reality of change by dating the statements you make.

Indexing Generalizations

Indexing is a companion skill to dating. Dating accounts for differences caused by the passing of time. Indexing accounts for the innate differences among groups of people, objects, or places. *Indexing* is the mental or verbal practice of accounting for individual differences.

Indexing counters the tendency to make sweeping generalizations. To some extent, generalization is an important part of our reasoning. It allows us to take what we have learned from one experience and apply it to another. When George tells the group that he got file cards, pencils, and paper at the campus store, Glenda is likely to go to the campus store for her supplies. When Sam notices that the group appreciates his participation today, he is likely to participate more actively the next time the group meets. When Marie learns that former leaders have been promoted for doing excellent work on her committee, she may try to improve her committee work. In these ways Glenda, Sam, and Marie use what they learn from one experience and apply it to another—they *generalize.*

Yet, misuse (or overuse) of this power can cause two serious communication problems. The first is the tendency to take the general characteristics of a class of people or objects and assign them to all the members within that class. For instance, because men (a class) in general have greater strength than women (a class) does not mean that Max (a member of the class of men) is stronger than Barbara (a member of the class of women). Or, the fact that a university is ranked among the top twenty in the nation does not mean that every department in that university is so ranked.

A second problem is the tendency to transfer a characteristic of one person (or object) to another person (or object) just because that other person (or object) is in the same class. For instance, because Klaus, a German, is industrious does not mean that all Germans are industrious or that Fritz, who is also German, is industrious. Similarly, just because one group can work four hours without a break does not mean that all groups can or should work four hours in a row without a break.

Now that we have considered the need for accounting for individual differences, let us see how the skill of indexing is used. Indexing calls for us to assign numbers to each member of a class. In the class of men we have man^1, man^2, man^3, and so forth. To illustrate how this works in a conversation, we'll make a statement that generalizes, followed by a statement that is properly indexed:

Generalization: Men are stronger than women; therefore, Max is stronger than Barbara.

Indexed statement: Men are in general stronger than women; therefore, Max is probably, but not necessarily, stronger than Barbara.

Generalization: The department must be good because the university is ranked among the top twenty in the nation.

Indexed statement: Because the university is among the top twenty in the nation, the department should be a good one, but it may not necessarily be.

Generalization: Fritz is likely to be industrious because Klaus, who is also German, is very industrious.

Indexed statement: Fritz is likely to have the same industrious nature as Klaus (they're both German), but Fritz could be different.

Generalization: Your group should meet for four hours before you need a break because Jerry's group was able to go for four hours without a break.

Indexed statement: Jerry's group met for four hours without a break. Yours might be able to do as well, but it may not.

In short, before you make a statement about something, consider whether your statement is about a specific object, person, or place or whether it is a generalization about a class to which the object, person, or place belongs. If you discover that your statement is not based on specific knowledge, inform your group of that fact. As a human being you cannot avoid generalizing but indexing your statements can help you avoid the problems that hasty generalization sometimes creates.

Citing Source Material

Another necessary information-sharing skill is that of citing source material. In any presentation in which you are using ideas that are not your own, you should acknowledge the source of the material in your remarks. Including sources not only will help the group to evaluate content but will add to your credibility as a researcher. In a written report, designate ideas taken from other sources by using footnotes. In group discussion, include acknowledgments in your statements. Your citation need not include all bibliographic information. Statements such as the following are appropriate in most instances:

> According to an article about Senator Hatfield in last week's *Time* magazine . . .''

> In the latest Harris poll cited in last week's issue of *Newsweek* . . .

> The conservative point of view was well summed up by William F. Buckley Jr. in his book *God and Man at Yale*. In the opening chapter, Buckley wrote . . .

> In order to get a complete picture we have to look at the statistics. According to the *Statistical Abstract,* the level of production for underdeveloped countries rose from . . .

> In a speech before the National Organization for Women given last fall, Billie Jean King said . . .

> During a personal interview last week, Raoul Gordon, a noted area cave explorer, said . . .

You do not want to clutter your remarks with bibliographical citations, but you do want to make sure that you have properly cited the sources of key information.

EXERCISES

1. Consider the following questions in your group:

a. Can American cars compete with foreign cars as economical metropolitan vehicles?
b. Is the dog man's best friend?
c. Does the end justify the means?

2. Have one-half of your group discuss a topic for five to ten minutes while the remainder of the group rates them on maintaining objectivity, dating, indexing, and using provisional statements. After the critique, observers and discussants should switch.

Organizing Information

The material presented for consideration in a group will, of course, correspond to the issues the group has agreed to discuss. As a group moves forward through the agenda, it is unrealistic to expect perfectly logical organization.

Study of groups in action shows that groups will digress, move back and forth from topic to topic, and at times go in unexpected directions. Students of group work have offered several models of how group procedure is organized. Let us consider a few of them.

One of the most widely used models of group communication is the three-phase model advanced by Bales and modified by Bales and Strodtbeck.[2] It suggests that with every topic (or issue) a group will experience three stages: (1) problems of orientation (discussing the nature of the situation), (2) problems of evaluation (voicing attitudes about the specific issue), and (3) problems of control (deciding what to do about each issue). Thus, according to Bales, if a group considers eleven issues or topics, the three-stage cycle will occur eleven times.

In 1965, Tuckman devised a four-phase model that synthesized the findings of others.[3] The stages have unique rhyming names: (1) forming (identifying an issue), (2) storming (expressing emotional responses to issue and content), (3) norming (developing group cohesion in relation to the point being considered), and (4) performing (arriving at a decision).

Schiedel and Crowell see the pattern of group communication as a spiral.[4] A member introduces an idea, another responds, and the original idea is extended, revised, questioned, and accepted or rejected. If the idea is rejected, the group starts over. If the idea is accepted, it provides a new ''anchor'' position from which the group works. The process of ''anchoring'' and ''reach-testing'' (reaching out with new ideas), is not linear, but cumulative.

By this discussion I don't mean to suggest that a group's procedure should not be organized. I do mean to show that even the best-organized groups will experience circling or spiralling activity. Group work is by nature inefficient at times, but as long as someone in the group works to keep discussion near the key issues, some digression is acceptable. As I stated in Chapter 3, the person who draws the group back to key issues when they have strayed too far is playing the role of expediter.

Responding to Information

What happens to the information presented in a discussion depends largely on how other members of the group respond to it. Responses can help the group mold well-substantiated decisions or can lead to the loss of vital information. Important responses that help clarify information are questioning, paraphras-

[2]Robert F. Bales and Fred L. Strodtbeck, ''Phases in Group Problem-Solving,'' *Journal of Abnormal and Social Psychology,* Vol. 46 (1951), pp. 485–495.

[3]Bruce W. Tuckman, ''Developmental Sequence in Small Groups,'' *Psychological Bulletin,* Vol. 63 (1965), pp. 384–399.

[4]Thomas M. Scheidel and Laura Crowell, ''Idea Development in Small Discussion Groups,'' *Quarterly Journal of Speech,* Vol. 50 (1964), pp. 140–145.

ing, and supporting. Inappropriate responses are those that are irrelevant, interrupting, tangential, incongruous, or evaluative. In this section we will look at each type of response. Because all response skills begin with and depend on listening, let us examine that important skill first.

Listening

No matter how many times we speak in a group, we are likely to spend far more time listening than speaking. Yet, of all our communication skills, we are most complacent about listening. We think that if our ears are normal, we can hear everything that goes on around us, but, in fact, listening and hearing are not the same. *Hearing* means registering the sound vibrations; *listening* means making sense out of what we hear. Research studies have shown that most of us listen with only 25 to 50 percent efficiency—that is, 50 to 75 percent of what we hear is never processed.[5]

To analyze listening, let us first consider the two characteristics of listening that are functions of heredity and environment: hearing acuity and vocabulary.

Some people have real hearing problems. Although accurate data are difficult to come by, authoritative estimates indicate that as many as 10 percent of adults have some hearing difficulty. If you know you have a hearing problem, you may wear a hearing aid or you may learn to adapt to the problem; but if you are not aware of the problem, poor hearing can limit your listening effectiveness. If you suspect that you have a hearing problem, you should have tests done at your school health service. The tests are painless and are usually provided at minimal or no cost.

The vocabulary of the listener is a second element of effective listening. If you know the meanings of all or at least most of the words you receive, you will understand what is said and you will have a good chance to retain much of what you hear. But if many of the words you hear are meaningless to you, your listening is bound to be affected. Many poor students have average or better than average intelligence but are handicapped by poor vocabulary. If you have a below-average vocabulary, you must work much harder to develop listening skills or must work to improve your vocabulary. You can help yourself by asking what a word means when you don't know. Many people pretend to know the meaning of a word because they feel foolish asking. It is difficult to call attention to your ignorance, but it is far more detrimental in the long run to act on information or respond to a person when you don't understand than it is to feel foolish for a moment. Listening and vocabulary are

---

[5]This original statistic, from Ralph Nichols and Leonard A. Stevens, *Are You Listening?* (New York: McGraw-Hill, 1957), pp. 5–6 , has been replicated several times.

related. Don't let your listening suffer because you are afraid to ask what a word means.

Although you may have some listening problems, you can improve your listening ability. The following suggestions can be helpful if you are willing to concentrate and practice.

1.   Get ready to listen. Listen efficiency increases when you follow the elementary practice of really being ready to listen. Getting ready involves your mental and physical attitudes. Mentally, you need to stop thinking about the thousands of miscellaneous things that pass through your mind. Direct all your attention to the speaker and to what he or she is saying. Daydreaming, or wool gathering as it is sometimes called, is a leading cause of poor listening. Physically, you need to assume a posture that keeps you alert. Because physical alertness encourages mental alertness, you may find it helpful to look at the speaker's face as he or she talks or to sit upright in your chair.

2.   Make a complete shift from speaker to listener. When you are planning to be a listener, it is relatively easy to get ready to listen. In group discussion, however, you may quite frequently switch from the speaker role to listener role. If you spend your time as a listener preparing your next speaking contribution, your listening efficiency will nose dive. We have all been in or witnessed situations in which two persons talked right past each other under the guise of ''holding a conversation.'' In comedy routines, such situations are often hilarious; in real life, the results of such ''communication'' are often pathetic. As you participate in your group, double-check what you are doing. Are you ''preparing contributions'' instead of listening? Are you making a complete shift from the speaker role to the listener role?

3.   Listen actively. If you let your mind wander or if you prepare contributions while you are supposed to be listening, your efficiency will go down. On the other hand, if you use your time to raise questions about the nature of the material, if you couple group information with your own experience, or if you mentally repeat key ideas or associate key points with related ideas, you may be able to raise your listening efficiency. We often think of the listening experience as a passive activity in which we are sponges soaking up information. In reality, good listening is hard work that requires concentration and a willingness to mull over what is said. If you have really listened during an hour-long group session, you may actually feel tired. That's good! It shows you have been working.

4.   Withhold evaluation. Do you ever find yourself turning off because of your emotional response to what is being said? Poor listeners are often given an emotional jolt when other group members invade an area of personal

sensitivity. When a person trips the switch to your emotional reaction, let a warning light go on before you go off. Instead of quitting or fighting, work harder at being objective. Good listening depends on comprehension. Withhold your evaluation of the message until you have the entire meaning.

Questioning Information

The appropriateness of your response depends on getting enough information. If in a discussion you are not getting enough information to work with, the most appropriate response is to ask for additional information.

You have, no doubt, been asking questions ever since you learned to talk, but you may occasionally find that asking a question irritates or flusters the other person. Defensive reactions usually result from the phrasing of the question. Let us first look at the most important goals of questioning; then we will discuss appropriate phrasing.

The first goal of questioning is to get more information—more details to clarify a general statement. For example:

Ann: I think I was most surprised by the amount of paper they use for their inter-office communication.

Nell: Do you know exactly how much they use in, say a month or a year?

Fred: If that isn't enough, Morgan asked for another supply report.

Sam: Will it have to be as long as the last one you wrote?

The second goal of questioning is to clarify the meaning of a word that is used:

Martha: He's just so sanctimonious.

Adelle: I don't understand. What do you mean by "sanctimonious"?

Phil: Parker's actions have been irresponsible.

Bob: What has he done that you see as "irresponsible"?

The third goal of questioning is to draw out a person's feelings about an issue:

Cal: What a day! Barton called this meeting when I was hoping to work on the monthly report.

Pete: Are you upset about having a meeting now?

Norm: Billy called. He's not going to be here.

Kay: Are you disappointed that he will miss the meeting?

To succeed as clarifiers, questions must be perceived as honest efforts to discover information that will help the questioner to understand. If a person perceives questions as actual or veiled attacks, his or her reactions are likely to be defensive. Suppose that in reply to Fred's statement about the supply report Sam had replied, "Well, you have to expect that kind of work; this is a profit-making business, you know!'' Fred might see this statement as an attack on his attitude about the job; thus the response would produce conflict rather than clarification.

When you need additional information to understand, ask a question. Determine the specific information you need, then phrase a question that will get the information without making a person defensive. Ask your question in a sincere tone of voice—not one that can be interpreted as sarcastic, cutting, or evaluative. Questioning should come out of a spirit of inquiry and support—not from a real or apparent need to make the person look bad.

Paraphrasing

Paraphrasing means restating the message you heard *in your own words*. Paraphrasing is the response that is most appropriate when you think you understand what a person means but (1) you are not absolutely sure or (2) you recognize that understanding is very important in the particular context. Some of the most serious communication problems in groups occur when members are ''sure'' they understand. The chance of misunderstanding is so great when four, five, or six others are involved that paraphrasing should be a working part of your group communication skills.

Paraphrasing is restating the message you hear in your own words, not just repeating words as in the following example:

Charley: I'm really going to study the report this time.

George: You're really going to study the report this time.

Such repetition shows that George has heard the words but it does not show that George really understands what Charley is saying. To paraphrase a message effectively, you should (1) listen carefully to the message—absorb every clue to the meaning, and (2) restate the message, this time in your own words. Let us try again on the same one-sentence statement:

Charley: I'm really going to study the report this time.

George: I take it that this time you'll read it several times and really think about its implications.

Charley: Well, at least more than once.

George's paraphrase shows what the words ''really going to study'' mean to him.

Perhaps you're thinking that George might ask, ''What do you mean by 'study'?'' To be sure, a sincere, well-worded question is appropriate when you are looking for additional information. But in this case, most people would think they know what ''really going to study'' means. George thinks he does. So George isn't looking for new information, he's checking to make sure that what he thinks ''really going to study'' means is the same as what Charley thinks it means.

When you paraphrase, concentrate on the content, on the substance of the message, or on the speaker's feelings about the message. All are appropriate considerations, depending on the situation. Let us go back to Charley's statement, "I'm really going to study the report this time." George's response is a paraphrase that focuses on content—it shows George's understanding of the substance, the meaning of "really going to study." If George had replied, "From the way you say that I think you're pretty upset with Barton's reaction to your preparation," he would have focused on George's feelings—on the possibility that George was upset.

This example is based on a one-sentence statement. Although you may find yourself paraphrasing single sentences, you will probably listen to several sentences before a paraphrase is appropriate. To illustrate, let us paraphrase a series of sentences:

Donna: Last week I sent the revised article to Carson. I was happy with my work because I felt the changes I had made were excellent. You can imagine how I felt when I got the article back yesterday with a note from Carson saying that this draft was not much better than the first.

Marcia: (Before continuing the conversation, Marcia wants to make sure that she really understands the stubstance of Donna's remarks.) If I understand, you're saying that the editor who read your revision said he could see no real differences, but you think your second draft was not only different but much better.

(Or, before continuing, Marcia wants to understand Donna's feelings about what she has just said.) From what you're saying about the situation I get the idea that you're really disappointed and hurt by Carson's failure to recognize the changes you made.

We usually don't differentiate between content and feeling paraphrases. A final example presents a paraphrase that combines content and feelings:

Marcia: If I understand, you're saying that Carson said he could see no real differences, but you think your draft was not only different but much better. I also get the feeling that what he said really irks you.

You may think that if people stated their ideas and feelings accurately in the first place, you would not have to paraphrase. But because of the intensity of group interaction, people are going to talk even if their ideas are not completely organized. Moreover differences in perception and uses of language make understanding difficult even when phrasing is good. So, in your effort to be a superior communicator in groups you must perfect the art of paraphrasing. Equally important is understanding *when* to paraphrase. Before continuing a discussion, paraphrase the ideas or feelings of another person when:

1. You are not sure you understand what he or she has said or how the person feels about what was said.

2. You need to better understand a message before you or the group can continue.

3. You perceive that what was said is controversial or was said under emotional strain.

4. You or the group have a strong reaction to what was said or how it was said and the strong reaction might interfere with your interpretation of the message.

Being Supportive

Being supportive means doing or saying something that shows sensitivity to the person speaking. Support shows: (1) that you care about the person, (2) that you empathize with his or her feelings, and (3) that you acknowledge the person's right to a feeling or a belief.

Nearly everyone in a group will show support at some time, but people often get so wrapped up in their own ideas that they may neglect to reward the contributions of others.

Support can be shown nonverbally with a smile, a nod, or a positive gesture. When Susan says, "We're straying from the point," and you agree, show some sign of agreement. A vigorous nod might be most appropriate. When you agree with a statement, you can show your support by sitting up straight and by not fussing, talking to a neighbor, or yawning.

More often than not, it is the verbal statement of support that is omitted. When Ann presents an accumulation of facts that obviously took her a long time to collect, say something supportive such as, "That's an impressive amount of material, Ann. You must have worked hard to collect it."

Responding Inappropriately

We have been looking at appropriate responses that clarify group communication. Inappropriate responses do just the opposite: they increase defensive reactions, they fail to confirm people or ideas, and they fail to keep interaction flowing.

A response that causes a defensive reaction threatens people and causes them to feel a need to protect themselves. A disconfirming response causes people to question their self-worth and undermines their self-concept. Responses that fail to further the flow of interaction are dysfunctional.

Some common inappropriate responses that tend to arouse defensiveness, to disconfirm, or to be dysfunctional include irrelevant responses, interruption, tangential responses, incongruous responses, and evaluative responses.

Irrelevant Response   An irrelevant response is one that is unrelated to what has been said—in effect, it ignores the speaker entirely:

Bob: Carson's explanation is clear enough, but I don't think it proves the point he's trying to make.

Tom: I've got some statistics from the personnel director that we might be able to use now.

When the sender is ignored, he questions whether he was heard and he begins to wonder about the worth of what he was thinking or saying.

Interrupting Response   Breaking in before the speaker is finished is an interrupting response:

Bob: Carson's explanation is clear enought, but . . .

Tom: I thought so, too. I appreciate it when . . .

People tend to interrupt when they believe they know what the sender is going to say, when they believe their own thoughts are more important, or when they are not paying careful attention. All these reasons show a lack of sensitivity to the sender. Humans need to verbalize ideas and feelings regardless of whether or not they are already known. Interruptions can damage the speaker's self-concept and make him or her hostile. Whatever you have to say is seldom so important that you have to interrupt the speaker. When you do interrupt, realize that you are lessening the speaker's effectiveness.

Tangential Response.   A tangential response is really an irrelevant response that is stated tactfully. With a tangential response, the receiver acknowledges hearing the speaker's statement, but the result, changing the subject, is the same:

Bob: Carson's explanation is clear enough, but I don't think it proves the point he's trying to make.

Tom: Well, that's your opinion. I've got some statistics from the personnel director that we might be able to use now.

Even though Tom acknowledges Bob's statement, Tom is saying that Bob's point is not important enough to deal with. Again, such responses chip away at the sender's feelings of self-worth. Bob is raising an issue that may be important to the group, but Tom ignores it.

Incongruous Response   Communication problems often occur when non-verbal messages conflict with the verbal messages. An incongruous response is an example of this kind of conflict.

Bob: Carson's explanation is clear enough, but I don't think it proves the point he's trying to make.

Tom: (in sarcastic tones) Yeah, it was really clear.

Tom seems to be acknowledging and verifying Bob's statement, but his sarcastic tone causes Bob to wonder whether he is confirming the ideas or making fun of them. Nonverbal messages generally override verbal messages, so Bob will probably react to the sarcasm. Tom's sarcasm and insensitivity to Bob's honest statement of feelings can cause a barrier to communication. And even if Tom is being sincere, barriers can grow as a result of Bob's confusion about Tom's meaning.

Evaluative Response People often reply with statements that evaluate the speaker or what he or she is saying. Evaluation changes the original issue, often creating a communication barrier:

Bob: Carson's explanation is clear enough, but I don't think it proves the point he's trying to make.

Tom: Questioning Carson's thinking is idiotic. He's the best economist we've got.

Tom's response is evaluative and changes the subject to a consideration of whether Bob makes idiotic statements. A barrier results because the statement is irrelevant but, more important, because it is an attack on Bob—an attack that probably will result in defensive behavior.

How can you avoid making inappropriate responses? First, listen to the other person. If you spend your time thinking of what you have to say, your response is likely to be inappropriate and you may give an irrelevant or interruptive response. If, on the other hand, you really listen to what is said, you are more likely to understand and acknowledge the idea or feeling the speaker is expressing. Second, be sensitive to the needs of the other person. Assume that what a person says is important to that person—even if it does not seem important to you. Take the idea or feeling at face value. If what the person has said is not, in your opinion, very important (or worth talking about) respond honestly with your ideas or feelings:

Bob: Carson's explanation is clear enough, but I don't think it proves the point.

Tom: I can see where you would be concerned if the point weren't relevant, Bob, but I think that Carson's point is right on target. What do the rest of you think?

Tom's response is honest and lets Bob know why Tom doesn't want to continue the discussion. Bob can accept Tom's opinion or the group's opinion or can try to persuade Tom and the group that his criticism is sound.

EXERCISES

1.

◆ Martin is listening as the group talks about an idea he has proposed. He did not spend much time on the proposal, but he thought it was a good one. Several members of the group are strongly criticizing his ideas. A look of dejection comes across his face, and in a trembling voice he says, "I never said this was a finished product—I was only giving you a sketch of an idea."

Members of the group make a number of responses. Label them as (A) questioning, (B) paraphrasing, (C) supportive, or (D) inappropriate:

a. "Will you give us some of the specifics you considered and show how they might work?"
b. "From the look on your face and the sound of your voice, I get the idea that you're uncomfortable with the group's comments."
c. "I sense that you weren't trying to give a comprehensive plan, and you're taken aback by the group's detailed comments."
d. "Martin, you know what they say, 'If you can't stand the heat, get out of the kitchen'!"
e. "I can understand why you might feel a little defensive, we've come down pretty hard on what you said."

2.

◆ Working in groups, discuss the questions raised in the last exercise. Half the group should discuss while the other half observes. Those discussing should ask questions, paraphrase, and support. Observers should consider when attempts were made, how well they were made, and when they should have been made.

3.

◆ Choose a question for discussion. Then assign the following roles:

> Gatekeeper
> Expediter
> Analyzer
> Clarifier
> Questioner
> Leader
> Supporter

One person can, of course play more than one role.

Discuss the topic question for twenty minutes. At the end, compare the recorder notes of each group. Discuss the amount of ambiguity, tension, and so forth.

4.

◆ Divide the class into six-person groups. Each person draws roles from a hat. Everyone, except recorder, may draw more than one role, and everyone may play information-giver and opinion-giver. However, no one may play other roles besides his or her assigned ones.

At the end of the discussion:

a. Have people guess who played various roles.
b. Discuss flow, ambiguity, tension, and so forth.

Summary

Talking in a group involves sharing information, responding to information, and organizing information.

Most of your participation in the group will be in sharing information and will involve giving and receiving information and opinions. Skills related to sharing information are maintaining objectivity, stating information provisionally, dating information, indexing generalizations, and citing sources.

What happens to information presented depends on how members of the group respond. Any response requires good listening. Clarifying is accomplished by asking for more information, by defining ideas, by drawing out feelings, by paraphrasing (stating your understanding of what the speaker means and how the speaker feels about what he or she says), and by supporting. Group members should avoid inappropriate responses such as ignoring, interrupting, responding incongruously or tangentially, or evaluating.

Although information presented may be organized around the issues the group determines to be vital to decision making, it is unrealistic to expect perfectly logical organization. The group is likely to go through various stages of development and to proceed in a spiral pattern.

8

MANAGING CONFLICT IN GROUPS

As a group works to achieve its goal, some conflicts are bound to occur. Conflict is the clash of opposing ideas and feelings. As with interpersonal conflict, the issue is not whether conflict will occur but what should be done about it when it does occur. Let us consider the nature of group conflict and the means of coping with it.

Nature of Group Conflict

Group conflict may be analyzed on the basis of its content, differences in values, and ego involvement.

Content Conflicts

Group conflicts often start with clashes over *content*. The conflicts are likely to occur in any of four sets of circumstances:

1. *The conflict may be over a fact.* For example, two or more persons in the group may come into conflict over the average number of hours children watch television each week.

2. *The conflict may be over an interpretation of a fact or an inference drawn from a fact or series of facts.* Two or more persons in the group may, for example, disagree over whether the rise in steel prices will trigger another round of inflation. The rise in steel prices may be documented as fact; what will result from that rise is a matter of opinion based on interpretation of the fact or on inference drawn from the fact.

3. *The conflict may be over a definition.* Two or more persons in the group may, for example, come into conflict over whether the use of communication strategies to motivate people to buy a product is unethical behavior or good salesmanship. In this type of conflict, the antagonists agree on what is being done; the problem lies in how each person defines the behavior.

4. *The confict may be over a choice among goals, actions, or means of arriving at goals.* Two or more persons in a group may, for example, come

into conflict over whether building a multilevel garage or using available space more efficiently is the better solution to the campus parking problem. Or they may come into conflict over the procedure they should use to make such a decision. In this type of conflict, the opponents agree on the problem but disagree on the solution.

Value Conflicts

Conflicts build and become more difficult to resolve as competing value systems are brought to bear on the issues. *Value conflicts* are differences in views of life in general (or of an aspect of life) that are brought into focus on a particular issue. Groups may seek, for example, to answer such questions as whether experience is more important than pay in an entry-level position or whether companies should provide recreational facilities for employees. The evaluative question concerning experience versus pay may result in a direct clash of values; the policy question concerning recreational facilities may result in clashes of values at various stages of the discussion.

An analysis of value conflicts requires discussion of the concept of values. In starting this discussion, I am struck with the observation that for more than 2,000 years the best minds in the world have wrestled with the significance of comparative values. Moreover, for the better part of a century, psychologists have studied human attitudes in an attempt to determine why and how we think, feel, and behave as we do. In the face of this history, I make no pretenses of presenting a comprehensive analysis of values in just a few pages. Still, the subject of values is so important to behavior in decision-making groups that we have to form some conclusions about the nature of values and about how they affect decision making.

Because values influence and are influenced by attitudes and beliefs, we will begin our discussion by defining the interlocking concepts of beliefs and attitudes. An *attitude* is a predisposition for or against people, places, or things. You can think of an attitude as a tendency or an inclination to feel or to believe a certain way. If, for example, I asked you "What's your attitude toward physical fitness?" you might say, "Very positive. Physical fitness is essential." In this case, your attitude would be favorable.

Whereas an attitude is a predisposition, a *belief* is an acceptance of an idea on the basis of evidence, opinion, and experience. So we can say that beliefs are outgrowths of attitudes. Although we may use the word "belief" rather loosely in conversation, we are likely to believe that something is true only if someone can prove it to our satisfaction. For instance. I might believe that keeping in good physical condition increases a person's chances of avoiding heart disease. My belief may be based on statistics and examples that I remember from reading various magazines. How are beliefs an outgrowth of attitudes? If I hold a favorable attitude toward physical fitness in general, it will be easier for me to establish a belief that being in good physical condition does, in fact, lower the likelihood of heart disease.

Let us come back to the subject of this section—values. A *value* is a cluster of attitudes or beliefs that serves as a guideline for measuring the worth of various aspects of our lives. We hold economic, esthetic, social, political, and religious values. A person's attitudes and beliefs may be either causes or results of economic, esthetic, social, or political values. For example, a person who believes in physical fitness may come to value a trim, solid, healthy body as a result. On the other hand, valuing a trim, solid, healthy body may lead to favorable attitudes and beliefs about physical fitness. Furthermore, the set of attitudes-beliefs-values a person holds about physical fitness will influence his or her perception of related topics—from smoking, to playing racquetball, to the company he or she prefers.

The values we hold are both societal and personal. A societal value that is important to most Americans is the worth of the individual. When the needs of government and the rights of the individual are in conflict, Americans are inclined to protect individual rights over governmental needs. Other societies have different values. In many Asian societies, for instance, the individual's rights are totally subsumed by the needs of the state.

In addition to societal values that shape most Americans' behaviors, each of us applies different personal values to individual events. For example, if Jack values educational opportunity more than he values personal wealth, he will be inclined to vote for a property tax increase for the schools. Tom, whose personal values are the opposite of Jack's, will be inclined to vote against the tax increase.

A value, then, is a frame of reference used to determine the relative goodness of any object, situation, or behavior. And it is in the framework of the group members' various operating value systems that decision-making questions are considered and ultimately decided. And these various operating value systems are likely to result in conflict.

Ego Conflicts

Group conflicts reach their height as disputants become ego involved in the outcomes. *Ego conflict* occurs when the persons in conflict view "winning" or "losing" the conflict as a measure of their expertise, personal worth, or image. Ego conflicts are particularly damaging to the interpersonal relationships of group members. Ego conflicts develop in the discussion of content elements or value judgments when one or both parties introduce personal or judgmental statements. For example, in a discussion of whether children under five watch more television than children over five watch, the simple content conflict may be escalated into an ego conflict when one or both parties see the issue as one of stupidity versus supreme knowledge—the eventual winner is the master of supreme knowledge and the loser is relegated to the role of a poor stupid individual.

Who you are, what you are, what competence you have, whom you should or do have power over, and how much you know arc somc of thc factors in the makeup of your self-concept. When a conflict is somehow tied to your personal worth, the conflict becomes an ego conflict. If you see yourself as an expert on the effects of television viewing, you may perceive a disagreement about how many hours people watch television as an attack on your self-esteem. Once your ego becomes involved in the conflict, your ability to cope rationally is often lost. Before you realize it, emotions become involved in the conflict, words are said that cannot be taken back, and the conflict gets blown out of proportion.

So we have seen that most group conflicts began as clashes over a fact, an interpretation, a definition, or a choice among goals, actions, or means of arriving at goals. These conflicts build as competing value systems are revealed and come to bear on the issues. The conflicts reach their height as disputants become ego involved in the outcomes. This is the nature of group conflict. How can people cope with group conflict?

Coping with Group Conflict

There is a wide range of behaviors for coping with group conflict. We will first look briefly at some common negative reactions to conflict; then we will focus on several of the more constructive ways of coping with conflict.

Withdrawal

One of the most common, and certainly one of the easiest, ways to deal with group conflict is to withdraw. *Withdrawal* is physical or psychological removal from the situation. Although disengagement may be useful under some circumstances, when withdrawal is a person's primary way of managing conflict, it is harmful.

Physical withdrawal is, of course, easiest to identify. For example, as the group begins discussion of a controversial issue, Bart, who anticipates conflict, simply leaves the group.

Psychological withdrawal may be less noticeable. In Bart's case, for example, as the group begins discussion of a controversial issue, Bart presents some of the information he has found. When one or two others offer information contradicting Bart's material, Bart quits talking and starts thinking about the date he has that evening. Members of the group may or may not perceive that he is no longer thinking about the subject with them. This behavior is psychological withdrawal.

Because neither physical nor psychological withdrawal comes to grips with the issues involved, they are not satisfactory means of coping with conflict.

Surrender

Another negative conflict management behavior is *surrender*. When the surrenderer senses conflict in the group, he or she chooses to give in immediately to avoid the conflict. The attitude of the surrenderer is that actions, goals, and choices are never worth arguing about.

For instance, Gail says, "I think we ought to consider alternate means of funding the project," and Marion replies, "I was really thinking we should work with the one that we've used in the past." When Gail sees a conflict developing she says, "Oh, no need to consider alternatives—go ahead with the old plan." The old method may not meet the group's needs, but rather than expressing group needs or considering the comparative advantages of various positions, Gail immediately gives in.

Sometimes a person who feels persecuted reacts with a martyr role, making comments that seem to say, "Do it your way—it's just not worth arguing about. I can bear the suffering." Even though other members of the group get their way, such surrender can be infuriating to those involved. In fact, it can often produce more conflict because those involved will not disclose or discuss their true thoughts.

Aggression

Another common reaction to conflict in a group is *aggression*. Through aggression, one person attempts to force another to accept his or her ideas. When there is conflict or the suggestion of conflict, the aggressor strikes out.

The mark of aggression is force, not rational deliberation. For example, Quinn says, "I think we've all gotten rather exhausted from this discussion. I suggest we think things through over the weekend and meet again Monday." Parker replies, "If you want your job Monday, you'll stay here until we're done today!"

Quinn's statement obscures the conflict and Parker's statement escalates it. Neither statement resolves or discusses the conflict. Such negative reactions can change simple conflict to ego conflict, which may grow into a power struggle. The greater the degree of escalation or withdrawal, the more complicated the conflict and the more difficult management of that conflict becomes.

Discussion

The key to successful management of conflict is *discussion*, the verbal weighing and considering of the pros and cons of the issues in conflict. But just saying "let's discuss this point" may not be enough to bring about open discussion. Let us consider the various attitudes and behaviors necessary to a discussion that will result in more constructive ways of coping with conflict.

Do not Fear Conflict   It is often the fear of conflict that brings about such negative responses as withdrawal and surrender. Conflicts are going to occur. But when conflict is approached properly, it can be a constructive force in the discussion. It forces a group to examine alternatives, and it forces the group to test its thinking. As a result, constructive conflict can help a group arrive at better decisions.

Strive for a Group-Centered Orientation   Each participant must consider discussion in terms of the impact on the total group, and not in terms of benefits to individual members. Because the group's goal is a quality decision that will be supported by the participants, group emphasis is a prerequisite to all deliberation. When a conflict does arise, you will want to try to view it from the group perspective.

Keep Discussion on the Specific Topic About Which the Conflict Occurs   We have already pointed out that conflicts often start on content levels. If the group can keep the focus of the discussion on those content levels, the chances that the conflicts will grow out of proportion are lessened. For instance, if you find yourself in a conflict over a fact, try to disengage until a source for verifying the fact can be found or until some guideline for selecting competing sources can be determined. Likewise, when the conflict is over an interpretation of a fact, an inference drawn, or a definition, collect supporting material that is related directly to the issue—in short, keep the conflict confined to the issue at hand.

   Some authorities refer to content conflict as "simple" conflict. Because facts can be looked up, inferences tested, definitions verified, and competing goals weighed and evaluated, the conflict can be confined to the specific issues and resolved rationally. Nevertheless, with many conflicts, competing value systems will be revealed and these will confound the conflict management.

Keep an Open Mind About Views That Differ from Your Own   Conflict can be lessened if participants can be open-minded rather than dogmatic in their view of new material. *Open-mindedness* is flexibility in the way a person processes information. Rather than seeing concepts in absolute terms, an open-minded person is willing to tolerate other sides and examine other information. Dogmatism is just the opposite. A dogmatic person clutches tenaciously to his or her value system and judges every event on the basis of how it fits into that value system. Highly dogmatic people take a narrow perspective of the way the world operates, are rigid in their thinking, and believe *only* those people who are in positions of strong authority. For example, suppose a topic question has religious ramifications. If two group members, a Baptist and a Catholic, for instance, are both open-minded, they can discuss the issues reasonably well. Open-minded people may be committed to certain beliefs or attitudes that grow from their value systems, but they are aware of the common ground that exists between what they believe in and what they reject. In discussion, they seek a middle ground between their positions in order to resolve the question. If group members are dogmatic, however, they focus on their differences. They view the controversy in terms of black and white and never see the shades of gray that lie between their two positions. As a result, management is nearly impossible and conflict escalates.

Your goal in decision making should be to open your mind as much as possible, so that you can look for the common ground on which some agreement can be built. The open-minded or low-dogmatic person compares and evaluates issues related to belief systems and accepts or rejects them according to merit, not values. Thus, the open-minded person looks for evidence and draws conclusions on the basis of the weight of that evidence.

Test Criteria Used in Making Value Judgments   We recognize that differing individual values will create conflict, especially when the group makes evaluations. Under these circumstances, it is necessary to seek an informative base for the evaluation rather than to rely on personal values. To illustrate, let us consider a question often discussed by film fans at Academy Award times: "What was the best movie of the year?" Without careful structuring, consideration of the "best movie" becomes a matter of personal taste reflecting personal values. It is vital for group members to identify criteria on which such a judgment may be based and to establish a way of testing those criteria. So, in keeping with guidelines for analyzing questions of evaluation, the group moves immediately to establishing such criteria as story, music, acting, directing, popularity, and so forth.

Next, and probably most important in managing conflicts, the criteria should be weighed to determine which are most important in making judgments. But this weighing should be made with some objective procedure. Walter and Scott[1] suggest four questions that can be asked about each criterion: (1) Has the criterion produced desirable effects in the past? (2) Have authoritative figures accepted this criterion? (3) Does the criterion fit the

---

[1]Otis M. Walter and Walter M. Scott, *Thinking and Speaking,* 3rd ed. (New York: Macmillan, 1973), p. 245.

needs of the group? and (4) Is the criterion justified by reasoning? These tests will not eliminate value considerations. Neither will they eliminate conflict—but they will lend structure to consideration of the issues and allow the group to make a decision based on information, not personal values. For example, by asking the question "Have authorities accepted this criterion?" group members can research film authorities' comments to see whether the criteria of story, acting, directing, message, and so forth are favored by the critics. If, for example, several critics cite "film message" as the major measure of film quality, the group can assign importance to that criterion in its evaluation of the year's movies.

Cooperate Rather Than Compete   When a conflict arises, variables that first affect the outcome of the conflict are the participants' competitive or cooperative attitudes. If attitudes are competitive, participants are likely to be ego involved. The alternative to the competitive attitude is the cooperative attitude. Cooperation is willingness to follow the steps of the problem-solving method we have considered throughout this textbook: (1) identifying the problem, (2) analyzing the nature of the problem, (3) suggesting possible solutions, and (4) selecting the solution that best meets the needs determined in problem analysis.

In some conflicts, one person may initially look at the outcome competitively while the other has a cooperative outlook. In this situation, the nature of the conflict will depend on whether the person looking at the conflict competitively draws the other person into the competition or whether the person looking at the outcome cooperatively influences the other person to cooperate.

If a person approaches the potential conflict competitively, how can you bring the person into a cooperative state so the conflict can be considered rationally? First, do not get into the elements of the issue at hand until you demonstrate to the other person that you wish to resolve the conflict in a mutually satisfactory way. Second, avoid any statements that escalate the potential conflict or result in defensive behavior. Some of the following wordings may be useful in demonstrating your resolve to be cooperative and in preventing an escalation of the conflict:

> I know you feel very strongly that what you believe is right. Before we consider whether your plan is the best one, perhaps we could consider what we want to accomplish with the plan.

> I know I sometimes get a little hotheaded in conflict situations, and I'm going to try to look at this problem as objectively as I can, but I may need you all to help.

You have good reasons for your belief, and I believe I have, too. Perhaps if we share our reasons and then consider their consequences, we can make a decision that is satisfactory to the entire group.

Developing a cooperative atmosphere takes practice. But you can learn to recognize when you start to become ego involved. At that time, mentally step back and ask yourself to problem solve. And when you see a colleague becoming competitive, you can perhaps paraphrase the feelings as well as the content of his or her message to determine whether the person is becoming competitive. For instance a statement such as, "From the way you're making your point, I get the feeling that this particular approach is very important to you personally."

Remember, your language, both verbal and nonverbal, indicates your feelings, not only about the conflict, but about the people with whom you are in conflict. If you approach members of the group openly and with respect, you should at least get a hearing, but if you demean a person's idea or the person himself by your words or actions, you are likely to create defensiveness, cause hard feelings, and escalate the conflicts.

Use Behaviors That Result in Positive Conflict Management   Each group participant is likely to have attitudes and feelings that determine the nature of his or her participation in the group. These attitudes and feelings may be classified as distributive or integrative.[2] A *distributive* approach is one in which a win-lose situation is developed—that is, if one person wins, it must be at the other person's expense. Conflicts that develop from viewing the situation as win-lose are negative and are difficult to deal with. An *integrative* approach, on the other hand, is one in which the members of the group believe that by integrating their resources to accomplish a common task, all members will prosper. A group playing poker may be contrasted with a group working a jigsaw puzzle to illustrate the difference between distributive and integrative approaches. In playing poker, an individual is working at the expense of others; in working a jigsaw puzzle, each person is working in cooperation with others.

The National Training Laboratories describe two opposite modes of behavior: one that results in negative conflict and one that avoids conflict or results in positive or useful conflict.[3] Let us look at five of the most important differences between these two modes of behavior:

---

[2]Based on an analysis made in the *1968 Summer Reading Book* of the National Training Laboratories Institute of Applied Behavioral Sciences, pp. 57–58.

[3]*1968 Summer Reading Book*, pp. 57–58.

Behavior that results in negative conflict	*Behavior that reduces conflict or results in positive or useful conflict*
1. Purposefully pursuing one's own goals.	1. Purposefully pursuing goals held in common.
2. Maintaining secrecy.	2. Maintaining openness.
3. Disguising or misrepresenting one's own needs, plans, and goals.	3. Accurately representing one's own needs, plans, and goals.
4. Being unpredictable—using the element of surprise.	4. Being predictable—using behavior consistent with past experience.
5. Threatening and bluffing.	5. Avoiding threats or bluffing.

Most group members have a reason or motive for behavior in a group that is, at the beginning of the meeting, unknown to other participants. Undisclosed reasons or motives for behavior are called a *hidden agenda*. For example: Tom wants to make sure the group will be finished by 3 P.M. so he can get to another meeting; Bill will go along with anything unless it is advocated or presented by Joan; Angelo is a member of another group that has a vested interest in a particular outcome of this group; Joan feels that she has been forced to take part and wants to get the job done quickly so she can get out of the group. The behaviors resulting from such hidden agendas can be used to illustrate the comparative modes of behavior listed above. If none of the participants reveals these hidden motives or reasons during discussion, we have secrecy instead of openness. If each person considers information in light of the hidden agenda, we have purposeful pursuit of individual goals as well as disguise and misrepresentation. The hidden agenda may be so overpowering that it alters a person's ordinary behavior. And to get his or her way, the person may threaten or bluff. Let us consider an alternate scenario. If at the beginning of the meeting Tom said, "I've got another meeting at 3 P.M., let's try to get finished by then. If we can't, either you can continue without me or we can meet again at another time," he would be establishing a base for an integrative approach. If each of the participants were to take such an approach, it is much more likely that their behavior would be positive and that their conflict management would be much better.

Practice Harmonizing Skills   A group cannot avoid some conflict, and if there is no one present to harmonize, participation can become an uncomfortable experience. Harmonizing skills involve making statements that help individuals work more cooperatively. Harmonizing may be recognized by such statements as, "Bill, I don't think you're giving Mary a chance to make her point,'' ''Tom, Jack, hold it a second. I know you're on opposite sides of this, but let's see how you might agree,'' ''Sue, I get the feeling that something Todd said really bugged you. Is that right?'' or ''Hold it, gang, we're really coming up with some good stuff, let's not lose our momentum by name calling.''

Prearrange Conflict-Management Procedures   Many of the difficulties of group conflict management arise because the group does not have procedure to turn to for coping with conflict. Just as groups who have made plans for what they will do in case of a fire, a flood, or a tornado often weather the particular disaster in much better shape than do those who have no such plan, so groups weather conflict better if they have a plan for conflict management.

Someone in the group will recognize that conflict is escalating. It is for that person to remind the group of the prearranged procedure. For instance, if the group has agreed to list advantages and disadvantages of conflicting actions before the conflict heats up, when such a conflict occurs, the prearranged procedure will take precedence over any actions. Sometimes the time involved in going through the prearranged steps is enough to get groups past that explosive moment when members are likely to say or do something they would like to take back later. Such prearrangement may not be practical at all times. But when a group anticipates a great deal of conflict with a given issue, such prearrangements might be a necessity.

Many of the guidelines listed in this section can be put together into a package that will serve as a conflict-management procedure. Following a plan encourages rational analysis to take precedence over emotional outburst. Fundamental to any plan is the possibility of negotiation. *Negotiation* means managing conflicts through trade-offs. Conflict often results when two actions are proposed but only one can be accomplished. A group cannot recommend hiring more police and, at the same time, recommend cutting back on the police budget, without negotiation. If the group believes that more police are needed and that the budget must be cut back, they can look for ways of cutting the budget that will still allow for additional hiring.

EXERCISES

1. ◆ Describe a conflict situation that arose during your group's deliberations.

2. ◆ Identify the kind of conflict it was.

3. Did those involved cope with the conflict by withdrawing, by surrendering, with aggression, or by discussing?

4. What was the outcome of the conflict?

5. If the outcome was negative, sketch a method of coping with the conflict that would have been more productive for both the individuals and the group.

Summary

When there is a clash of opposing ideas or feelings, conflict occurs. Conflicts in groups are likely to begin as content conflicts over facts, interpretations of facts, definitions, or choices. Conflicts build as competing value systems are revealed and are brought to bear on the issues. Conflicts reach their height as disputants become ego involved.

Conflicts may be coped with in a variety of ways. Negative behaviors include withdrawal, surrender, and aggression. Positive behaviors include problem-solving discussion. In discussion, participants restrict conflict to the subject, keep an open mind, test the criteria for value judgments, cooperate rather than compete, and use behaviors that result in positive conflict management.

9

DRAWING CONCLUSIONS IN GROUPS

Everything that we have considered thus far—determining goals, analyzing, researching, discussing, and coping with conflict—culminates in the final stage of decision making—drawing group conclusions. So whether the question for consideration is as narrow as whether the public relations program should be eliminated, or as broad as what the major priorities of the marketing division during the next fiscal year should be, there will be a number of conclusions drawn during the course of the deliberation.

In this chapter we will look at the foundation of drawing conclusions, the reasoning process. We will then recommend specific ways to draw conclusions about causes, alternatives, and conflicts. We will examine the major danger in the process of drawing group conclusions, groupthink. Finally, we will consider the important task of recording group decisions.

Reasoning

William Minto wrote: "We can look at facts—over them, under them, around them, and not be a whit the wiser unless we can reason with and from those facts."[1] Nowhere is this more true than in group decision making. Regardless of the kind of question, the group must be able to reason logically in order to arrive at the best decisions.

Reasoning is the process of drawing inferences from facts or of proving statements with facts. Suppose you are concerned with what is happening in your group. As you think about it, you say to yourself, "Nearly everyone has missed several important meetings. Those who do participate don't seem particularly well prepared, and the group seems more willing to spend time on unrelated topics than to concentrate on the question to be resolved." From these observations you conclude, "We've lost our commitment." You have reasoned by drawing an inference, a conclusion, from the data.

Now suppose that at the next group meeting you present your view. You say, "Well, to tell you the truth, I think we've lost our commitment." You go on to say, "Look, we've all missed several important meetings, during dis-

---

[1]Arthur N. Kruger, *Modern Debate* (New York: McGraw-Hill, 1960), p. 132.

cussions no one seems particularly well prepared, and we seem to look forward to getting off the topic.'' This, too, is an example of reasoning, but in this case the conclusion is presented first and the facts are given in support.

Whether you draw inferences from facts or form arguments with facts in support, you are reasoning. With both approaches you need a method of examining the process. The method suggested here is to analyze the process on the basis of three essentials: the data, the conclusion, and the warrant. To conduct this analysis, you must prepare a diagram of the process. (Although I present a rather traditional analysis of the types of reasoning here, I will show the nature of the process using the diagrammatic method developed by Stephen Toulmin.[2])

Data are the evidence, assumptions, or assertions that provide the basis for a conclusion. In the previous example, the data were missed meetings, lack of preparation, and willingness to be sidetracked. The *conclusion* is the product of the reasoning, the inference drawn, or the inference to be proved. In the example, the conclusion was ''We've lost our commitment.'' The *warrant* is a statement denoting the substantive relationship between data and conclusion. Now, you will need to think carefully about the warrant because it is the key that shows how the conclusion follows from the data that have been presented. The warrant is usually implied rather than stated; however, before you can test the soundness of the reasoning, the warrant must be stated. If you find that you cannot word a sentence that shows how the conclusion follows from the data, the reasoning may be fallacious. How might the warrant be stated for the example cited above? You could say that missed meetings, lack of preparation, and willingness to be sidetracked are all indications or signs of loss of commitment.

To examine reasoning critically, you may find it valuable to write the entire example down so that you can look at each part carefully. Using (D) for data, stated or observed, (C) for conclusion, (W) for warrant and an arrow to show the direction of the reasoning, the above example could be written as follows:

(D) Missed meetings; ————————————→ (C) The group has lost
       lack of preparation;   its commitment.
       willingness to be sidetracked.

(W) (These occurrences are indications
        or signs of a loss of commitment.)

The warrant is written in parentheses because it is implied rather than actually

[2]This analysis is based on the ideas set forth by Stephen Toulmin, *The Uses of Argument* (Cambridge, England: Cambridge University Press, 1958).

stated. The warrant, then, indicates how we arrived at the conclusion from data supplied.

So far, you have seen how a unit of reasoning can be diagrammed. Now you need to see how the essentials can be tested in order to judge the validity of the reasoning.

You can apply two tests to reasoning. First, you can use the tests of evidence outlined in Chapter 6. Then you can test the logic of the warrant by casting it in the form of a yes or no question: "Is it true that missed meetings, lack of preparation, and willingness to be sidetracked are indications of loss of interest?" If the answer is "Yes, a high percentage of the time," the reasoning is sound; if the answer is "No" or "Rarely," the reasoning process is fallacious.

Analyzing reasoning schematically in the data-conclusion-warrant framework does not ensure the infallibility of the logic. However, if you take the time to write out the process in this manner and ask whether the warrant is supported by research, the chances of discovering illogical reasoning are increased considerably.

Although a number of different kinds of warrants can be phrased, most of the kinds of reasoning you will do before or during your decision-making group discussions fall under five headings: generalization from examples, causation, analogy, sign, and definition. Let us look at each.

Generalization Warrants

A *generalization warrant* says that what is true in some instances is true in all instances (or at least in enough instances to validate the generalization). Although exceptions to generalizations can and do occur, they do not necessarily invalidate the generalization. However, if exceptions prove to be more than rare of isolated instances, the validity of the generalization is open to serious question. The following illustrates reasoning from examples to generalization: The group is investigating athletic financing. Jed says, "I've got information from Miami University, Ohio University, and University of Cincinnati, and they all lost significant amounts of money last year. As far as I'm concerned, athletic programs in Ohio schools are a losing proposition!" Let us examine the reasoning schematically:

(D) Miami University, Ohio ───────────► (C) Athletic programs at
       University, and University   Ohio universities are
       of Cincinnati lost significant   losing propositions.
       amounts of money on their
       athletic programs last year.

                (W) (What is true in representative Ohio
                     universities is true in all Ohio universities.)

A generalization warrant may be tested by asking three questions:

1.   Are enough instances cited? Are Miami University, Ohio University and University of Cincinnati enough of a sample? Because instances cited should represent a significant sampling, enough must be cited to satisfy the listeners that the instances are not isolated or hand picked. In this case, three is not enough to draw such a generalization. The group will need data from at least two or three more examples.

2.   Are the instances typical? "Typical" means that the instances cited must be similar to or representative of most or all within the category. If instances are not typical, they do not support the generalization. Are the three Ohio universities typical of all universities in Ohio? In this case figures would need to be obtained from Ohio State University, the largest of the schools, and from schools such as Akron and Youngstown, which have smaller budgets. It may be that it is only the universities of a certain type in which athletic programs are a losing proposition.

3.   Are negative instances accounted for? Are there athletic programs in Ohio that did not lose money? Negative instances by themselves may not invalidate a generalization, but if negative instances are numerous and typical, no valid generalization can be drawn from the original ones cited.

Causation Warrants

Causation warrants are special kinds of generalizations in which one or more of the circumstances listed always produce a predictable effect or set of effects. As our hypothetical group continues to talk about athletics, the subject turns to the importance of winning teams. Pat says, "We're going to have a better record next year. Almost all of our best players will be back, the coach had an excellent recruiting year, and our schedule is easier." Pat is reasoning by causation. Let us examine her reasoning schematically:

(D) Best players will be back; ⟶ (C) We will have a better
      excellent recruits; easier schedule.   record next year.

      (W) (Returning best players, excellent recruits,
            and an easier schedule are causes
            of, or will result in, a better record.)

A causation warrant may be tested by the following questions:

1.   Are the data alone important enough to bring about the particular

conclusion? Are returning best players, excellent recruits, and an easier schedule by themselves important enough to result in more victories? If the data are truly important, eliminating the data will mean eliminating the effect. If the effect can occur without the data, we can question the causal relationship.

2.   Can other data besides the data cited account for the effect? Are other factors (such as quality of coaching, luck, and injuries) more important in determining the number of victories a team will have? If accompanying data appear as important or more important in bringing about the effect, we can question the causal relationship between cited data and conclusion.

3.   Is the relationship between cause and effect consistent? Do good players and an easy schedule always (or usually) yield more victories? If there are times when the effect has not followed the cause, we can question whether a causal relationship exists. In this case, the consistency would seem high, but it is certainly not guaranteed. From the data cited we could conclude that a better season is likely, but such a conclusion is far from certain.

Analogy Warrants

Analogy is another special kind of generalization. Reasoning by *analogy* attempts to show that similar circumstances produce similar conclusions. A warrant in the form of an analogy might be stated, "What is true or will work in one set of circumstances is true or will work in another, comparable set of circumstances." Our hypothetical group is considering means of bringing more revenue into the state to eventually help higher education. As they consider options, the subject of off-track betting comes up (placing bets on horse races by telephone, without having to be at the track). Tony says, "You know, off-track betting is generating money for New York, and because New York and Ohio are pretty similar, I think off-track betting would work in Ohio, too." Tony is reasoning by analogy. Let us look at this argument in schematic form:

(D) New York is making money ⟶ (C) Ohio would make
     from off-track betting; Ohio   money from off-track
     and New York are similar.   betting.

   (W) (Because off-track betting makes money
        for New York and because New York and Ohio
        are similar, Ohio would make money from
        off-track betting.)

An analogy warrant may be tested by asking the following questions:

1.   Are the subjects being compared similar in all important ways? Are New York and Ohio similar in form of government, in capability of handling betting, or in attitudes of residents? If subjects do not have significant similarities, they are not really comparable. New York and Ohio are both industrial eastern states with many similarities.

2.   Are any of the ways that the subjects differ important to the outcome? Is Ohio's difference in size and population from New York a factor? Is the difference in types of population a factor? If differences exist that outweigh the subjects' similarities, conclusions drawn from the comparisons are not necessarily valid.

Sign Warrants

A *sign warrant* is a kind of argument based on indications. When events, characteristics, or situations always or usually accompany other unobserved events, characteristics, or situations, the observed events are called *signs*. A sign warrant might be stated: "When one variable that is usually or always associated with another variable is observed, we can predict the existence of the other, unobserved variables." Signs are often confused with causes, but signs are indicators, not causes. A fever is a sign of sickness that occurs when a person is sick, but it does not cause the sickness. Let us look at another example: As the group begins, Laura says to Jed, "The way your eyes are watering and you're sneezing, I'd say you have a pretty bad cold." Laura's reasoning can be shown as follows:

(D) Eyes watering; sneezing.——————➤ (C) Jed has a bad cold.

(W) (Watery eyes and sneezing are
        signs of a cold.)

A sign warrant may be tested by the following questions:

1.   Do the data cited always or usually indicate the conclusion drawn? Do watery eyes and sneezing always (or usually) indicate a cold? If the data can occur independently from the conclusion, they are not necessarily indicators. Watery eyes and sneezing may also indicate an allergy or a sudden change in some condition.

2.   Are there enough signs? Are watery eyes and sneezing enough to indicate a cold? Events or situations are often indicated by several signs and if there are not enough signs the conclusion may not follow.

3.   Are contradictory signs in evidence? Is Jed bouncy and enthusiastic? If signs that usually indicate different conclusions are present, the stated conclusion may not be valid.

Definition Warrants

The four warrants just described are usually considered the major forms of reasoning, but people also reason from definition. A *definition* is a verbal classification that follows the application of specific criteria for that classification. A definition warrant is usually stated, "When a situation has all the characteristics that are usually associated with a term, we can use that term to describe the product of those characteristics." For example, after a meeting, three members of the group are talking about problems with the group. Laura wonders about the leadership. Nancy says, "I think Bill is an excellent leader. He takes charge, he uses good judgment, and his goals are in the best interest of the group." Nancy's reasoning can be shown as follows:

(D) He takes charge; he uses good ⟶ (C) Bill is an excellent
    judgment; his goals are in the   leader.
    best interest of the group.

   (W) (Taking charge, showing good judgment, and
       considering the best interests of the group
       are the characteristics most often associated
       with excellent leadership.)

A definition warrant may be tested by these questions:

1.   Are the characteristics mentioned the most important ones in determining the definition? Are taking charge, good judgment, and sensitivity to group goals the most important criteria of excellence in leadership? If the data presented are not usually considered criteria for the classification, the definition does not follow.

2.   Is an important aspect of the definition omitted in the statement of the definition? Do we need to consider Bill's influence or power? His desire to lead? If items that are ordinarily part of the definition are missing, the conclusion does not necessarily follow from the criteria listed.

3.   Are the criteria best labeled by some other term? Are taking charge and using good judgment better labeled by "autocrat" rather than "leader"? If another label fits the criteria better, the conclusion is not valid.

EXERCISES

1.

♦ Following are some typical examples of reasoning that you are likely to encounter in your groups. Indicate which items are based on reasoning by (G) generalization, (C) causation, (A) analogy, (S) sign or (D) definition.

_____ The garden club held a raffle, and they made a lot of money. I think we should hold a raffle.

_____ K&X didn't declare a dividend last year; I think they're in financial trouble.

_____ Maybe that's the way you see it, but to me, when high city officials are caught with their hands in the till and when police close their eyes to the actions of people with money, that's corruption.

_____ If interest rates hadn't gotten out of hand, I think the building industry would have recovered.

_____ The last three years' December profits put us ahead of the year before—I think we can plan on an increase this year as well.

_____ Candy is personable, highly motivated, and willing to travel— I think she'll make a good sales rep.

2.

♦ For each of the above draw and fill in a schematic. Write appropriate warrants.

3.

♦ Working in groups, discuss the relative strengths of each of these examples of reasoning.

Drawing Conclusions about Causes—Force-Field Analysis

You may recall that one of the most important aspects of resolving a policy question is to determine the nature, the extent, and the causes of the problem. The force-field approach may be highly beneficial to you in this stage of analysis because of its graphic display of the complexities of the problem.

Kurt Lewin[3] borrowed the force-field concept from the sciences. *Force-field analysis* presumes that the current situation is the way it is because sets of counterbalancing forces are keeping it that way. The causes of the problem may be viewed as the interaction of impelling and constraining forces. Conducting a force-field analysis requires the group to identify those forces that impel and those forces that resist change. A graphic display of these forces shows upward arrows representing the impelling forces for change and downward arrows representing the constraining forces resisting change. Later in the discussion, various solutions can be evaluated, in part, on how they might cope with these interactions.

[3]Kurt Lewin, ''Frontiers in Group Dynamics: Concept, Method and Reality in Social Science,'' *Human Relations*, Vol. 1, 1947, pp. 5–41.

Let us illustrate this analysis with an example. State University has commissioned a group to resolve the question of whether the university should adopt a semester calendar (instead of the quarter calendar currently used). By lising impelling and constraining forces, the group can begin to determine the interaction. The analysis would be shown as follows:

Constraining forces (against changing to semesters):

1. Shorter courses—if a student or faculty member doesn't like a course, it will soon be over.
2. Smaller units—courses can be given for ten weeks when they may not warrant fifteen weeks.
3. Convenient vacations.
4. Tradition.
5. The disruption of a change—some courses would have to be combined, some dropped.

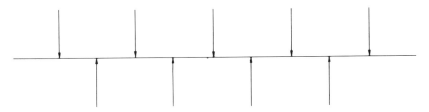

Impelling forces (for changing to semesters):

1. Two registration periods are better than three.
2. Two sets of grades are better than three.
3. Fifteen weeks gives more time for mastery of material.
4. Fewer courses could be taken.

As shown, this example represents a state of equilibrium. The five constraining forces hold the four impelling forces at bay. What would alter the equilibrium and bring about a favorable attitude toward the semester calendar? The impelling forces could be increased in number or intensity or the constraining forces could be decreased in number or intensity. In examining the example, we see that two weak constraining forces would appear to be numbers 2 and 3.

Let us consider number 2, smaller units—courses can be given for ten weeks when they may not warrant fifteen weeks. The quarter system apparently presupposes that most courses must be three hours. But, a three-hour quarter course could become a two-hour semester course. There would be the same number of hours of instruction; moreover, three quarter-hour credits and two semester-hour credits are the same administratively.

Now let us look at number 3, convenient vacations. The major vacations in a quarter system are Thanksgiving, Christmas, and Easter or spring break.

But a semester system can start at a time that will allow the term to end before Christmas, preserving the traditional Christmas vacation.

When these two constraining forces are weakened, the impelling forces outnumber and outweigh (have greater intensity than) the constraining forces. The end result is force toward the semester system.

In using a force-field approach, the first step is to identify the competing forces—to put them down on paper so they can be seen. The second step is to weigh them to determine the point of equilibrium. The group can then attempt to increase or decrease the number or intensity of the competing forces.

Force-field analysis is especially useful when a group has decided in favor of what they consider a superior course of action but must determine a way of implementing it that would win approval. For instance, suppose you were considering the question "What should be done to increase compliance with no-smoking rules in various parts of the plant?" By identifying the competing forces, weighing them, and considering strategies for increasing the number or intensity of impelling forces or for decreasing the number or intensity of constraining forces, you could reveal means of gaining compliance.

EXERCISES

You are a member of your school's scheduling committee. At your school there is a greater demand for courses between the hours of 10 A.M. and 2 P.M. than between 8 A.M. and 10 A.M. or 3 P.M. and 5 P.M. Your committee has been assigned the following question: "What should be done to increase student demand for classes between 8 and 10 A.M. and 3 and 5 P.M.?"

1. Prepare a force-field analysis of the problem. Write down your impelling and constraining forces as illustrated by the example on p. 123.

2. Develop a strategy to recommend to the administration based on an increase or decrease in the number of forces or an increase or decrease in the intensity of forces.

Brainstorming

Good decision making is information based. That is, given the discovery of all or most of the relevant information, a high-grade decision is likely to follow. Although most information is produced through research, information can be generated by participants. A group can create new ideas or new directions. Such generation may be accomplished by brainstorming.

Brainstorming is the process of stating ideas spontaneously with no attempt to evaluate the ideas as they are mentioned. The philosophy of brainstorming is that within an atmosphere of complete freedom, participants, through free association, can release creative processes and generate ideas that later can be sorted, developed, and evaluated.

Let us illustrate how such a process works in a decision-making group. Mary is leading a group of five people in resolving the question "What are some good ideas for a senior class present to the university?" The group has considered criteria for the selection. As the group reaches the point where recommendations are in order, it finds that it has only a few ideas to work with. At this point, Mary says, "I've asked Suzy to sit in for a few minutes to record ideas we come up with. In the next ten minutes or so I want each of us to say any idea that comes to mind, regardless of how wild it may sound. Our only purpose is to see how many ideas we can come up with."

Although the ideas may come slowly at first, within a minute or so all members should be contributing. The first few ideas will trigger others, people will begin adding on, and for a while ideas will come so fast that the recorder will hardly be able to keep up. An outsider should take notes to avoid interrupting the flow of ideas from participants. The same end can be achieved by tape recording this portion of the discussion. After the session, Mary might say, "We'll type up the list and get copies to you later this afternoon. If you have any afterthoughts, add them to your list, and we'll meet tomorrow to begin processing what we've got." If the group is pressed for time, a secretary could get the list of ideas typed up within the hour.

This example illustrates getting ideas, but you can use brainstorming whenever the group needs to come up with just the right idea, word, name, or whatever.

Why does brainstorming work so well? Basically, because it follows psychological principles of human behavior. Because no one, under any circumstances, is allowed to disagree, evaluate, or in any way comment on the value of an idea, quantity begins to develop. One way of breaking the primary tension that inhibits freedom of thought and expression is to have a high level of agreement. If a member who feels uneasy, unsure, or bashful makes a statement and receives agreement (or at least no disagreement), he or she is likely to be motivated to make another statement. Soon, members can forget themselves and their tensions. In a few minutes, brainstorming can develop a climate that facilitates complete freedom of expression.

Nominal Group Method

The assumption that underlies the theory of group decision making is that given time, information, and motivation, a group can arrive at a mutually desirable decision. Yet, there are times when emotions, events, competing values, or other forces make it nearly impossible for a group to work things out following the methods we have considered thus far. Under these circumstances a group could agree to disagree and report to the parent group that it can reach no agreement. Before admitting failure, however, I recommend that the group try what has come to be called the nominal group method. As you will see, the method is rigid, technical, and in some ways against the spirit of group consideration. On the other hand, the method has proven its worth in coping with apparently insurmountable conflicts and in achieving solutions the entire group can back. First, let us see how it works.

The *nominal group method* is a type of silent brainstorming in the company of a group. It is a listing procedure that involves three stages: (1) the individual listing stage, (2) the coordination stage, and (3) the ranking stage. Let us examine each step:

1. *Individual listing stage.* In this stage each person in the group works alone to prepare a list of ideas that relate to the issue being considered. If in resolving the question of how university departments can deal with retrenchment, that is, cutting back on faculty, courses, and services in the face of declining enrollments and revenues, the group came up with the idea of cutting clerical help, the group could use the nominal group method to determine the advantages and disadvantages of such a procedure. Each person in the group would prepare a list of ideas under the two headings of advantages and disadvantages. While the lists were being prepared there would be no discussion—each person would work alone.

2. *Coordination stage.* The second stage provides a procedure for disclosure of the information on the lists. The chairperson asks each group member, in turn, to disclose one item from the list. As each person makes a disclosure, the chair records it on a chalkboard. The sharing continues until each person's list is exhausted. On the topic of cutting clerical help, Gayle, the leader, might begin by asking Paul to list one advantage. If Paul says "Not lose faculty," any other person who has listed that advantage would cross it from his or her list. When the group finishes the list of advantages, it may have eight, ten, twelve, or even more possibilities. When everyone's list of advantages is exhausted, the group moves on to disadvantages.

3. *Ranking stage.* After all the advantages and disadvantages have been listed, each group member ranks the top five. The group's rankings are computed, and the chair lists the five advantages and disadvantages that have gained the greatest number of votes. By using such a method, the group can eventually identify what are perceived by the group as the major advantages and disadvantages. The group may stop its deliberations at this point, or they

may go on to discuss each item. Thus, although the method is a group method, it takes advantage of individual thought.

The nominal group method produces several benefits. First, the group can generate a list without haggling. Because the individual listing stage is a kind of silent brainstorming, it brings the same advantage as brainstorming: the inclusion of ideas without pre-evaluation. Moreover, the listing method allows both the advantages and the disadvantages of the proposal to be considered. It begins a counting and weighing procedure. Second, the nominal group method provides a means of determining group preference. It works on the basis of collective judgment. If four of the six members of your group think that certain advantages or disadvantages outweigh others, the collective opinion will be shown with the ranking. Moreover, the ranking helps focus later discussion on substantive points. Third, since everyone has equal opportunity to share views, the method works to reduce conflict.

The nominal group method may not be used often, but when impasses are reached, it can be a valuable way of proceeding.

Dangers of Groupthink

Throughout this textbook I have offered ideas that can and should be used by group decision makers to ensure the best possible decisions under any circumstances. The time seems right to consider one last guideline. Any group needs to understand the potential problem of groupthink and to formulate a procedure for preventing the groupthink phenomenon from short circuiting the decision-making process.

What is *groupthink*? Basically, it is a group attitude or norm that discourages or prevents airing of views that are counter to the majority views. It concerns the pressures for conformity of thinking that develop within a group regardless of the outcome or consequences of such conformity. Irving Janis is credited with identifying this tendency and labeling it groupthink. The basis for groupthink is the "safety of acting in numbers" phenomenon that allows groups to do things that perhaps no individual in the group would do alone or suggest in private. Mob mentality is a kind of groupthink—a bizarre idea is supported or bizarre behavior is advocated because it appears to be a group idea.

You have perhaps heard of the Asch experiments in which students were given the task of comparing the length of one vertical line with the lengths of three others. The subject of the experiment sat in a group of several "confederates" who agreed unanimously on the comparative length of the line. Although the agreement was unanimous, the group's assessment was purposely wrong. Asch noted that three-fourths of the students tested yielded to the unanimous judgment of the confederates on at least one of the trials and that one-third of the students agreed with the confederates on at least half of the trials.[4]

Uniformity is most likely to be seen when a group experiences pressure for consensus—total agreement on an issue. Sometimes this means conceding if you are the only one looking at an issue differently; sometimes it means following the lead of a person with high status, the most powerful or most trusted member of the group. Uniformity does not always result, and people with strong resistance can even affect majority views.

Janis outlines several circumstances under which groupthink is likely to occur.[5] Among them he lists (1) a shared illusion of invulnerability by group members which often results in excessively risky decisions, (2) collective efforts to rationalize the group's decision and to discount the thinking of dissidents, (3) an unquestioned belief in the group's inherent morality, (4) direct conformity pressure brought to bear on dissenting members to bring their opinions into line with those of the majority, (5) self-censorship by individuals of doubts they may have about the wisdom of the group's decisions, (6) a shared illusion of unanimity about judgments that conform to the majority view, and (7) the emergence of self-appointed mindguards who protect others in the group from information that might lead the group to question the effectiveness and morality of their decisions.

Various authors have suggested guidelines that groups can and should follow to ensure against groupthink. The following are some of the most important:

1. Allow sufficient time for discussion. Too often, a key or vital decision is introduced at or very near the scheduled ending time of the meeting. Pressure then exists to resolve the issue regardless of the lack of time. It is amazing how often a group will allow itself to make a hasty decision because time is short. If you see such pressures building, do what you can to put off resolution until there is more time. Quick decisions are too often made in the groupthink mode.

2. A climate should be developed that allows for freedom of speech regardless of how ridiculous a point may sound at the moment. The whole point of group decision making is to allow all to look at the issues from as many points of view as possible before a decision is made.

3. Criticisms should be made of ideas rather than of persons. If persons

[4]S. E. Asch, "Effects of Group Pressure upon the Modification and Distortion of Judgments," in H. Guetzkow (ed.), *Groups, Leadership and Men,* (Pittsburgh: Carnegie Press, 1951).
[5]I. L. Janis, *Victims of Groupthink: A Psychological Study of Foreign-Policy Decisions and Fiascoes* (Boston: Houghton Mifflin, 1972), pp. 198–199.

fear that they, instead of their ideas, will be attacked, they will be less likely to contribute ideas.

4. Every idea should be probed. No idea should be accepted at face value without some discussion.

EXERCISES

1.
Brainstorming
Select a question for discussion that involves creating a list of alternatives. Use the brainstorming method to develop the list.

2.
Nominal group method
For the same question, reach your goal by using the nominal group method. What were the advantages and disadvantages of each of the methods?

3.
Were there any evidences of groupthink in either of the discussions? If so, how did you deal with them?

Recording Group Decisions

People's perceptions and memories differ. In a one-hour group discussion, about 9,000 words will be spoken. When the one-hour meeting ends five members will have five separate perceptions of what took place. According to statistics on listening comprehension, the group will be able to recall 50 percent of the discussion—but what 50 percent? How many decisions will the group have made? Unless special effort is made to record the group procedure and decisions, much of the value of a one-hour discussion can be lost.

I have seen groups meet for one hour and agree on several points. A few days later when the group meets again, I've seen members question what they originally agreed on. Some members will express views that oppose earlier decisions. For this reason, a decision-making group needs a record of accomplishment. In formal group meetings this record is called "minutes." A recording secretary can follow guidelines from a book on parliamentary procedure such as *Roberts Rules of Order*. He or she records motions, key debates, and votes taken, and types them for circulation to the group members prior to the next meeting. The minutes then become a public record of the group's activity.

What happens in a small decision-making group? The leader may keep informal notes, but they may not provide an accurate record. Effective group decision making requires a good record of proceedings to:

1.   Have a formal statement of the group's accomplishments. Statements such as ''In the early portion of discussion the group decided to limit its analysis to activity in the southeastern states where declines in sales have been noted'' summarize what took place and apprise every member of the group of the decision. If some controversy arises later, the group can be reminded of the decision.

2.   Have a record of all intermediate decisions that lead to and supply a basis for the major decisions. In the chapter on analyzing questions we noted that every major question depends on answers to key subquestions. Unless the group can provide information that leads to the major decisions, the group's process is open to question. Parent groups or other organizations cannot rely on blind faith that the group made a comprehensive analysis of the question. A record of decisions shows others what was done.

3.   Protect against misunderstanding and misperception by individual members. Statistics on listening tell us that, as time goes by, people recall less and less of what was said unless they are reminded. At the end of a day's meeting you may be able to summarize key decisions and key information. Three weeks later, what happened is likely to be a blur. You may even alter the wording of key points or may transpose information.

4.   Act as a running account of group process. The first three reasons show the importance of a record after the meeting is over, but a record is also important when the group is in progress. At any point in the discussion, a member should be able to find out where the group is, whether the discussion fits the group goal, or what foundation is being built on new information. A careful written analysis during the discussion can furnish the necessary information. Good discussion is and should be a slow process, but anything that can be done to make the process more efficient without detracting from the necessary spontaneity should be encouraged. A written account keeps what is happening in front of the group and avoids ambiguity.

Ways to Record

There are several ways that group record keeping can be accomplished. The size of the group, the complexity of the issues, and the potential resources can help you determine which method to use.

Audio-visual Recording   Audio visual recording appears to be the ideal method of record keeping because every word is preserved. Your group, however, may find the method totally impractical because someone will have to listen to the entire tape and record points that were made. Second, while listening, the person may discover that at certain key places the group did not arrive at any decision that achieved group consensus. In this case, the group would have to reconsider that particular point. And third, unless the group ''performs'' it is likely that some key thoughts will be lost along the way. There is nothing wrong with using this method as a back-up if the group wishes, but it is not likely to be the best way.

Leader Record Keeping   Record keeping by the leader is the most common method in decision-making groups. In many groups, the leader has an informal responsibility to report the findings of the group. Because the leader's role is less likely to be one of information giver or opinion giver, he or she can more easily focus on such roles as summarizing, drawing conclusions, and testing the wording of conclusions. The leader can keep a running record and check for consensus in wording or content. However, a problem may occur because the leader holds a high-status position, so group members may not be willing to press the leader into stating key decisions that are reached. Furthermore, the leader may interpret the group's meaning rather than confirming the wording of a decision with the group.

Rotating Recording   To rotate recording, each member of the group takes a turn recording. This is probably not the best method for several reasons. First, some people will be better recorders than others, and the record will be erratic. Second, it is difficult to correlate record-keeping with individual interests. When a person has a lot to contribute, he or she will not want to be recorder or will feel inhibited in the discussion.

Delegated Recording   Because the recorder role may be best accomplished by a person who is not deeply involved in content, the group may want to appoint someone or ask for a volunteer who is not ego-involved in the content of the day's work. If your group has the resources, it may want a recorder who is not a part of the group. Doyle and Strauss of Interaction Associates cite several good reasons for this, including the point that recording takes commitment, and if a person is trying to contribute to or facilitate the discussion, making an accurate record becomes quite difficult.[6] For class exercises, I recommend that one person per group be assigned the recorder role to learn the skill—a skill that is as important as any other skill demonstrated within the discussion.

[6]Michael Doyle and David Strauss, *How to Make Meetings Work* (New York: Wyden Books, 1976), p. 126.

How to Record

1.   As recorder, you should have a copy of the agenda or the procedure that the group has agreed to. Although the group may stray from the written plan, you will still have some idea of what is going to happen or what should be happening, and your note-taking will be made easier.

2.   Briefly note key information as it is presented. It is a good idea to make note of what each person says.

3.   When a key question is answered, record the answer in full and underline or star it. Read it back to the group so that the group recognizes when it has arrived at a key decision and so it can double-check wording.

4.   Record too much rather than too little. You do not need to type up everything, but it is much easier to cut out material than it is to add information that you find difficult to remember.

5.   After the meeting, type up and duplicate the notes and circulate them to group members before the next meeting.

Doyle and Strauss recommend that the recorder write notes on large sheets of paper taped to a wall or a chalkboard so that members of the group can see exactly what is happening at all times. The same thing can be accomplished by a person sitting with the group and taking notes. Every person has the right to ask the recorder to read the last decision made or to read back a summary of information.

As with any other skill, good recording takes a great deal of practice. You will find that when a person gets good at the job, the entire group prospers.

EXERCISE

Choose a question for discussion. Have each person play the role of recorder until some conclusion is reached. At the end of the total discussion, compare the individual records.

Summary

The culmination of group deliberation is the drawing of conclusions. Reasoning is the process of drawing inferences from facts or proving inferences with facts. The essentials of reasoning are the data, the conclusion, and the warrant, a statement that demonstrates the relationship between the data and the conclusion. Some of the most common warrants are generalization, causation, analogy, sign, and definition.

Force-field analysis presumes that the current situation is the way it is because sets of counter-balancing forces are keeping it that way. Conducting a force-field analysis requires the group to identify impelling and constraining forces. By reducing or enlarging the number or by decreasing or increasing the intensity of the impelling or constraining forces, the group can determine strategies for implementing solutions.

During deliberation a group will have occasion to rely on a number of supplementary processes in their drawing of conclusions. Brainstorming is the process of spontaneously stating ideas with no attempt made to evaluate ideas as they are mentioned. Brainstorming can generate a great number of ideas in a relatively short period of time.

The nominal group method is a type of silent brainstorming that involves listing, ranking, and coordination of ideas by group members. Although the nominal group method is rarely used, it may be just the approach for those times when an apparent impasse is reached.

Groups should make every effort to avoid groupthink, the attitude or norm that discourages or prevents airing of views that are counter to majority opinion. Groupthink may best be countered by allowing sufficient time for discussion, by developing a climate that allows for freedom of speech, by criticizing ideas rather than persons, and by probing every idea presented.

A group needs written documentation of its decisions. The group may keep an audio-visual record or a written record kept by the leader or a delegated recorder. The record should include the key issues of the agenda, brief notes of key information, and answers to the key questions. At the end of the meeting, the written record should be duplicated and circulated to group members.

Readings for Part Two

Freeley, Austin J. *Argumentation and Debate,* 5th ed. Belmont, Calif.: Wadsworth, 1981. See especially: Chapter 1, "Reasoned Decision Making," and Chapters 6 and 7 on evidence.

Gouran, Dennis S. *Discussion: The Process of Group Decision-Making.* New York: Harper & Row, 1974. The chapter on discussion questions provides alternate procedures and questions for analysis.

Hare, A. Paul. *Handbook of Small Group Research,* 2nd. ed. New York: Free Press, 1976. Excellent summary of data on various aspects of the decision-making process.

Johnson, David W., and Johnson, Frank P. *Joining Together.* Englewood Cliffs, N.J.: Prentice-Hall, 1975. Includes a number of group exercises.

Kahane, Howard. *Logic and Contemporary Rhetoric,* 3rd ed. Belmont, Calif.: Wadsworth, 1980. An excellent source for reviewing reasoning and fallacies. Its emphasis on practical application of logic can be easily adapted to group deliberation.

Patton, Bobby R., and Giffin, Kim. *Decision-Making Group Interaction,* 2nd ed. New York: Harper & Row, 1978. Especially good is the section on problem solving.

Scheidel, Thomas M., and Crowell, Laura. *Discussing and Deciding.* New York: Macmillan, 1979. Outlines a step-by-step movement through the group process.

Shaw, Marvin E. *Group Dynamics: The Psychology of Small Group Behavior,* 3rd ed. New York: McGraw-Hill, 1981. An excellent synthesis of research findings on group process.

Tubbs, Steward L. *A Systems Approach to Small Group Interaction.* Reading, Mass.: Addison-Wesley, 1978. Although much of the material complements the content of this text, its focus is much different.

Filley, Alan C. *Interpersonal Conflict Resolution.* Glenview, Ill.: Scott, Foresman, 1975. Contains a great deal of material that is relevant to managing group conflict.

THREE

LEADING GROUPS

Decision making requires effective leadership. In this two-chapter unit,
we will examine theories of leadership and discuss the
responsibilities of an effective leader.

10

LEADERSHIP THEORIES

Leadership means many things to many people. To some, it is an inherent, almost divine complex of traits that sets one person apart from his or her peers. To others, it is the lucky providence of being in the right place at the right time. Even among researchers, definitions of leadership differ from source to source. Yet common to most definitions are the ideas of influence and accomplishment.[1] In short, *leadership* may be defined as exerting influence to accomplish specific goals.

Within most of us is a deep feeling that whatever leadership is, we have what it takes. Although it is fashionable to talk publicly about how we ''wouldn't take the job of leader for all the tea in China,'' in private we may see ourselves as the only logical candidates for the job. Nevertheless, leadership in decision-making groups is not something that can be thought of lightly. The goals of this chapter are to examine the source of influence in leadership and to look at leader traits, leader styles, and interaction models.

Social Power

The ability to exert influence to affect the attitudes and behaviors of others occurs only under certain clearly definable circumstances. For real leadership to occur there must be a relationship between the potential leader and those being led. Your group will be motivated to respond to your leadership attempts only if they perceive that you have some power over events, circumstances, and the people involved. Effective leadership grows from or is based on a real or perceived social power base.

What is social power? *Social power* is the potential for changing the attitudes, beliefs, and behaviors of others. The presence of power does not ensure support, but the absence of power makes it nearly impossible for people to accept leadership.

Several social psychologists have offered analyses of social power. The one that seems to make the most sense in understanding group interaction is

---

[1]Marvin E. Shaw, *Group Dynamics*, 3rd ed. (New York: McGraw-Hill, 1981), p. 317.

French and Raven's analysis describing the bases of social power: coercive power, reward power, legitimate power, expert power, and referent power.[2]

Coercive Power

Coercive power derives from the potential to punish. Coercive power can be physical or psychological; it can be actual or threatened force. The elements of coercion are size, strength, and possession of weapons. If we remember the definition of power as the *potential* for change, we can see that a person can have coercive power without attempting to exercise it. The old vaudeville joke "Where does a gorilla sit when he comes into a room? Anywhere he wants to" illustrates the effect of this potential.

Most often coercive power is used as a threat. You may attempt to coerce your little brother into acting in a specific way by threatening to hit him if he does not. A mugger attempts to coerce his or her victim to hand over money by threatening to use a gun, a knife, or a club. A supervisor may attempt to coerce an employee with the threat of an undesirable assignment or involuntary termination. Each of these represents exercising of coercion by threatened punishment. Coercion works when the person being coerced perceives the demanded action to be less harmful to him than the threatened punishment. Coercion fails as a means of exerting influence if the person perceives the demanded action to be more painful than the threatened punishment. Jack Benny, who built his comic image on miserliness, brought about one of the longest laughs in entertainment history when he responded to the threat "Your money or your life" with a long pause followed by, "Just a minute, I'm thinking." If your little brother decides that getting hit is less painful to him than taking a bath, he just may take the punishment—if he can't run faster than you can.

How effective is coercion as a means of exerting influence in a group setting? If "effective" means getting the desired result, coercion can be very effective. If, however, it means getting the desired result in a way that is likely to improve the group relationship, coercion is likely to be quite ineffective. It is human nature, for those of us who are not masochists, to resent the threat of punishment. Some individuals become so resentful at the threat of even mild punishment that they would rather subject themselves to brutal hardships than submit to even an implied threat of force. Others who comply because of their distaste for the threatened punishment are likely to resort to revenge—to look for any way possible to strike back. Coercion often has overtones of brute force—and most of us believe that if a person's only way

---

[2]John R. P. French, Jr. and Bertram Raven, "The Bases of Social Power," reprinted in Dorwin Cartwright and Alvin Zander (eds.), *Group Dynamics*, 3rd ed. (New York: Harper & Row, 1968), pp. 259–270.

of exerting influence is through force, he is unworthy of our compliance in changing beliefs, attitudes, or actions.

Coercive power is not a part of effective, ethical influence in groups. Any of the following four bases of power is far more compatible with ethical group influence.

Reward Power

Reward power derives from the ability or potential ability of one person to bestow monetary, physical, or psychological benefits on another person.

Reward power is most often used as a motivator to change attitudes, beliefs, or actions. You may offer to reward your little brother if he will take a bath. Your instructor can reward you with a good grade for good work in his or her course. Your girl friend or boy friend may attempt to motivate you to do something by promising you a special gift for your birthday, for Christmas, or for Valentine's Day.

Reward power works as a means of exerting influence if: (1) the person sees the reward as large enough or important enough to compensate for the effort of the action called for, and (2) the person believes the one who promises has the power to give that reward. For example, if you offer to reward your little brother with ice cream for taking a bath, he may decide that the treat is too small a reward for enduring the pain of such an extensive cleanup. If you offer him all the ice cream he can eat, he may doubt your financial resources to do what you say you will do. Your instructor offers to reward good work with an A in the course. If you believe that the time and effort involved are more than you care to expend, the A might not arouse enough motivation in you; or, if you regard grades as unimportant, you are unlikely to make the effort to do the work.

How effective is reward as a means of exerting influence in the group setting? Compared with coercion, reward is a much superior motivator. We are more likely to be motivated to work by promise of reward than by threat of punishment. In this context, the reward is seen as a positive element. Ballplayers work hard to have a good season in hopes of the reward of higher pay; students work hard in classes in hopes of the reward of high grades. To be effective, the reward must be perceived as large enough or important enough.

Under some circumstances, reward power may be regarded negatively. If, for some reason, you do not believe a person has a legitimate motive for offering a reward, or if the person is offering the reward for actions that are objectionable to you, or if you do not respect the person offering the reward, you may reject the offer, reject the reward, or seek to bring down the person or agency misusing the reward power. Reward power is least effective when it is seen as bribery by one who chooses not to be bribed. Bribery, by definition, is a reward offered for questionable motives to do questionable deeds. Most of us, if we believe the offer to reward is made as bribery, are likely to resent it.

Legitimate Power

Legitimate power derives from the potential for influence gained as a result of election, selection, or position. The rationale for bestowing legitimate power is the belief that people in certain positions have the *responsibility* of attempting to exert influence. The president, senators, and members of Congress gain legitimate power through the ballot. Teachers, cabinet members, and committee chairmen gain legitimate power through appointment. In families the father and mother, the oldest child, or the oldest male child may have legitimate power because of tradition or cultural norms.

If a person is perceived to hold power legitimately, we are likely to cooperate with his or her attempts to exercise that power. It is OK for the chairman of a meeting to ask you to stop talking in order to aid the group effort; it may not be OK for one of the other members to ask you. It is OK for the coach of the team to pressure a player to change his or her style of play; it may not be OK for another player to do so. It may be OK for the oldest child to give the other children chore assignments; it may not be OK for the second oldest child to do so.

The extent to which a person will be influenced by the exercise of legitimate power often depends on factors other than the legitimate power itself. For instance, if the leader is perceived as powerless to enforce demands, a member of the rank and file may ignore the call to act. In this instance, the rank-and-file member may doubt the reward or coercive power potential accompanying the leader's legitimate power. Or a citizen may not do what the president or a member of Congress asks because the citizen has no respect for these leaders.

Probably the most important benefit coming to one who has legitimate power is the right to exercise other means of influence that are not perceived as OK when exercised by a person who does not hold legitimate power. You are likely to take more from your instructor because he or she has the legitimate power to conduct procedures in your particular class. As a result of this legitimate right, you give your instructor more leeway in, for example, criticizing your term paper than you would permit a person without the legitimate right.

Expert Power

Expert power derives from the potential to influence based on superior knowledge in a certain field. Expert power is present when you admit that another person holds information in a particular field that you need. Your instructor has the potential for expert power in your class because he or she has knowledge and expertise that you need. A coach has potential for expert power because he or she has knowledge and expertise that players seek. You, likewise, have the potential for expert power in several areas that you know well—perhaps cooking, playing tennis, or repairing automobiles.

People use expert power by attempting to influence others through the promise of revealing information. A coach influences his or her players when he or she reveals information that the players perceive as useful in their efforts to master a sport. A professor influences his or her students by revealing information about a subject that the students perceive as useful in their education. Expert power fails to influence when people do not believe that the information is useful to them, when they do not believe that the alleged expert does, in fact, have the relevant information, when they do not believe that the expert is able to disseminate that information in a usable manner, or when they believe that they have gained parity of information with the expert. An important element of expert power is that its potential exists only within the limited area of expertise. The tennis coach may hold expert power over her players on the subject of tennis but not on the subject of calculus.

How effective is expert power? It seems to be quite effective within its limited scope. However, because information can be exchanged, once a person believes that he or she has received all the information there is to give, the expert loses the effect of his or her power. Moreover, expert power must be real to be effective. For example, if one of your friends works as an auto mechanic in a dealer's garage, he has the potential to influence your choice of sparkplugs. If, on the basis of the mechanic's opinion that XYZ sparkplugs are superior, you purchase them for your car only to discover two months later that they have burned out, you are not likely to accept your mechanic friend's advice again. He has lost his expert power as far as you are concerned.

Sometimes people use their expert power as a weapon. They may purposely withhold information in order to maintain control over others. If a person believes that another is manipulating him or her with use of expert power, the expert may lose that power.

Referent Power

Referent power derives from the potential to influence others simply because people identify with the one who influences them. Many persons have power because of qualities that cause others to love and trust them. *Charisma* is a word used to label this power. Whatever you wish to call it, people acknowledge and yield to power residing in certain persons for no apparent reason beyond belief in the individual.

Not only does referent power stand on its own as a potential for influence, but it underlies the value of the other bases of power we have considered. Expert power, legitimate power, reward power, and even coercive power have greater potential for influence if the powerful person is also perceived as having referent power. Moreover, if a person doubts the referent power, he or she is less likely to be influenced by any of the other types of power.

A group leader, then, is likely to be perceived by members of the group as having a potential for influence based on coercive, reward, legitimate, expert, and/or referent power.

Although we have considered each of these bases of power separately, in most cases the power a person holds is a result of a combination of the various types of power.

EXERCISE

Decide whether each of the following statements is an attempt to influence based on coercive power (C), reward power (R), legitimate power (L), expert power (E), or referent power (Rf).

_____ 1. You will wear the kind of clothes that befit your position in this company because I'm your boss and I'm telling you to.

_____ 2. After a careful analysis of the statistics covering a number of years of sales patterns, I have concluded that . . .

_____ 3. Listen Bart, if you can get that report in before the first, I'll see to it that you get my backing for the chairmanship.

_____ 4. Listen, we've worked together for a long time— trust me—I can do it.

_____ 5. Jack, you'll get it done—if you know what's good for you.

Leadership Traits

What kind of person is most likely to be the leader of a group? Are there such things as "leadership traits" that, if discovered within a person, will predict his or her success as a leader? Although researchers have at times downplayed the presence of verifiable leadership traits, during the last decade there have been renewed research efforts in this direction.[3] Paul J. Patinka is but one researcher[4] who has substantiated Shaw's claim that there is enough consistency among individual traits and leadership measures to draw generalizations.[5]

---

[3]John F. Cragan and David W. Wright, "Small Group Research of the 1970's: A Synthesis and Critique," *Central States Speech Journal,* Vol. 31 (Fall 1980), p. 202.
[4]Paul J. Patinka, "One More Time: Are Leaders Born or Made?" in James G. Hunt and Lars L. Larson (eds.), *Crosscurrents in Leadership* (Carbondale, Ill.: Southern Illinois University Press, 1979), pp. 36–37.
[5]Shaw, p. 325.

What conclusions have been drawn? Leaders exemplify traits related to ability, sociability, motivation, and communication skills to a greater degree than do nonleaders. As far as ability is concerned, leaders exceed average group members in intelligence, scholarship, insight, and verbal facility. In sociability, leaders exceed other group members in regard to such things as dependability, activity, cooperativeness, and popularity. In motivation, leaders exceed other group members in initiative, persistence, and enthusiasm. And finally, people with the kinds of communication skills outlined earlier in this book exceed average group members. Remember, this does not mean that the person with superior intelligence in the group, or the one who is most liked, or the one with the greatest enthusiasm will necessarily be the leader. It does mean that a person is unlikely to be the leader if he or she does not exhibit at least some of these traits to a greater degree than other group members.

Do you perceive yourself as having any or many of these traits? If you see these traits in yourself, you are a potential leader. Because several individuals in most groups have the potential for leadership, who ends up being the leader depends on many things other than possession of traits.

EXERCISES

1. What do you believe are your strongest leadership traits?

2. In your discussion groups, discuss your opinions about the relative importance of various leadership traits.

Leadership Styles

The way a person handles himself or herself is called *style*. A casual examination of groups in operation will reveal a variety of leader styles. Some leaders give orders directly; others look to the group to decide what to do. Some leaders appear to play no part in what happens in the group; others seem to be in control of every move. Some leaders constantly seek the opinions of group members; other leaders do not seem to care what individuals think. Each person will tend to lead a group with a style that reflects his or her own personality, needs, and inclinations. Although people have a right to be themselves, an analysis of operating groups shows that groups work better or feel better about the work they have done if the style of leadership has been appropriate.

What are the major leadership styles? Which is best? In a pioneer study,

White and Lippett described three types of leadership behavior.[6] In effect, their analysis described a kind of continuum of leadership. At one extreme is the authoritarian leader, who maintains total control; at the other extreme is the laissez-faire leader, who for all practical purposes is a nonleader. Between these two extremes is the democratic leader. Few people's leadership styles fall consistently into any of the three categories White and Lippett describe; moreover, few people behave consistently in all situations.

If we go back to our definition of leadership—exerting influence to get things done—we can see that by definition an effective style is one in which the leader takes an active role in the discussion in order to influence its outcome. If that is the case, why isn't the authoritarian style the ultimate form of leadership? Although there are situations where authoritarian leadership may, in fact, be most desirable, it fails to meet the definition of leadership because it denies the value of group members. Let us explore characteristics of leadership style a little more deeply.

The authoritarian leader exercises complete control over the group. Authoritarian leaders determine the statement of the question, they make the analysis of procedure, and they dictate how the group will proceed to arrive at the decision. They are likely to outline specific tasks for each group member and to suggest the roles they desire members to play. They also praise or criticize individual contributions and determine the final decision with or without the help of the group.

The laissez-faire leader, on the other hand, does little but organize the group and supply information and material when asked. Laissez-faire leaders do not take part in, or even suggest directions for, group decisions. The group itself has complete freedom in determining every aspect of the decision-making process. Laissez-faire leaders are nonleaders.

Somewhere between these two extremes lies the ideal of democratic leadership. Democratic leaders *suggest* phrasing of the question, *suggest* procedures, and *suggest* tasks and roles for individual members. Yet in every facet of the discussion, democratic leaders encourage group participation to determine what actually will be done. Everyone feels free to offer suggestions to modify the leader's suggestions. What the group eventually does is determined by the group itself. Democratic leaders may exert influence at various times; that is, they may give reasons for the procedures they suggest. And the group may decide that the leader's suggestions are in its best interests. But in the final analysis, it is the *group* that decides. So, democratic leadership is not wishy-washy, it is not laissez-faire; neither is it authoritarian.

[6]Ralph White and Ronald Lippitt, "Leader Behavior and Member Reaction in Three 'Social Climates,'" in Dorwin Cartwright and Alvin Zander (eds.) *Group Dynamics,* 3rd ed. (New York: Harper & Row, 1968), p. 319.

What are the results of these leadership styles? The following analysis considers White and Lippitt's conclusions but includes others' research to verify, supplement, and occasionally modify their conclusions.[7]

1.   More work is done under a democratic leader or under an authoritarian leader than in a laissez-faire setting. When a group is directionless, it tends to flounder. So, the laissez-faire style is least effective under all circumstances. This is very important to note for at least one additional reason: when leaders who tend toward authoritarianism try to be more democratic, they often become laissez-faire. Many people just can't seem to lead without controlling. Thus, when they give up control, chaos reigns. Thus, laissez-faire is not to be confused with democratic leadership.

2.   More work is done under an authoritarian leader than under a democratic leader. Whether this is true most of the time or only some of the time is open to some question. According to Shaw,[8] either the authoritarian group is more productive or there is no significant difference. This means that if the sole criterion of effectiveness is getting a job done quickly, the authoritarian style of leadership is usually more effective and seldom, if ever, less effective than the democratic style.

3.   Work motivation and originality are better under a democratic leader. Evidence for this conclusion is quite consistent. In a democratic group, the members have a "piece of the action." They feel as if they have been active in the decision-making process. As a result, individual members are more likley to blossom under democratic leadership. Not only is individual growth potential the greatest, but individuals feel better about the group process. In most group settings, this is an important consideration.

4.   Authoritarian leadership seems to create aggression and discontent, even though the discontent may not appear on the surface. This is a companion conclusion to number 3. Again, research substantiates this point. Note that under an authoritarian leader, members may not be vocal with their discontent during the group process. In fact, an authoritarian group often gives the impression of complete harmony. But discontent, although below the surface, manifests itself in many ways. Discontent may be demonstrated by grousing in informal comments after the meeting about what took place during discussion, by footdragging in commitment to putting the groups plan into action, by abandonment of the group decision if the going gets rough during implementation, or by an indifference or hostility about taking time to work with the group.

[7]White and Lippitt, p. 334.
[8]Shaw, p. 279.

5. There is more dependence and less individuality in authoritarian groups. Whereas democratic leadership may help the individual to blossom, authoritarian leadership seems to stifle the individual. Because the authoritarian leader is quick to exercise coercive power, everyone looks to the leader to see what to do and how to do it so there will be no "mistakes." As a result, there is little likelihood that individuals will be willing to take initiative. Moreover, if the leader is absent for any reason, the authoritarian-led group tends to flounder. Members are not used to assuming leadership in authoritarian groups.

6. There is more group-mindedness and more friendliness under a democratic leader. Stated another way, people enjoy the group process more when they work under a democratic leader. They often look forward to meetings, get caught up in the group action, become oblivious to time, and look back on the group activity as a positive experience.

Analysis of the literature indicates that most researchers favor democratic leadership. Yet there are times when the democratic way is not the best choice. Participatory democracy has its limits. For instance, during a closely contested basketball game the coach who calls a time-out has one minute to help his players handle a particular defensive alignment the other team is using. He will not use his minute in democratic processes—asking his players if they have any ideas or suggesting a plan and giving the players the opportunity to evaluate it. Instead, the coach will tell the players how to proceed, make a substitution if he needs to, and give the players encouragement to do what he tells them. When the accomplishment of the task is or appears to be more important than the feelings of the members, authoritarianism may be appropriate. (This is not to say that a basketball coach or any other leader who adopts the authoritarian style for the moment can disregard group feeling.) As studies have shown, a job gets done as fast or faster, and often with fewer errors, under an authoritarian leader than under a democratic leader. Authoritarian leadership also seems to work well when the authority is superior in knowledge and skill to the participants. The basketball example bears this out. The coach is the coach because of what he knows. As long as the players respect his superior knowledge, they will work under the authoritarian style.

There is at least one other favorable aspect of the authoritarian form of leadership—it is easier. Learning to be a good democratic leader sometimes ends in the frustrations of laissez-faire nonleadership. In other words, some people confuse democratic leadership with no leadership. Since there is little ambiguity in authoritarian leadership—the leader gives directions and the group follows them—it is far easier to understand and administer.

If authoritarian leadership is your thing—and many authoritarian leaders do exist, are effective, and even win the approval of their groups—perhaps it would be well to consider one other point. The best authoritarian model seems to be "benevolent dictatorship." If the authority arises from the need to control—and perhaps to even crush dissent—authority leads to tyranny. But even an authoritarian leader can be likable. Even though authoritarianism is an approved model in coaching, the tyrant is seldom successful. Any group process is partly inspiration, and inspiration is seldom nurtured in a climate of hate.

EXERCISES

1. ◆ What is your leadership style? What have been the strengths and weaknesses of that style?

2. ◆ What kind of leadership style do you work best under? Why?

3. ◆ Compare your answers with those of your group.

Interactionism

So far, we have considered aspects of leadership as independent variables. However, research in the last several years has emphasized the joint effects of many factors. Shaw has called these many multidimensional approaches "interactionism."[9] The three variables that most often interact are the leader, the group, and the situation. Recently, Hollander (1978) took what he called a transactional approach, permitting leaders and followers to "engage in a process of social exchange in which each both gives and receives rewards or benefits."[10] However, aside from the observation that research is consistent with the transactional view, there has been little done with the theory that would give a leader or a potential leader insights into procedure.

The approach that has received the clearest explanation and has generated the greatest amount of research is Fiedler's *contingency model* of leadership effectiveness.[11] Fiedler's work provides at least two benefits in the study of leadership behavior. First, it clarifies the variables that interact, and second, it gives guidance in determining whether a task (or structuring) style or a

[9]Shaw, p. 334.
[10]Shaw, p. 334.
[11]Fred E. Fiedler. *A Theory of Leadership Effectiveness* (New York: McGraw-Hill, 1967).

maintenance style is most likely to be effective. Notice that his view of leadership style is slightly different from the ones we considered earlier in the chapter. Fiedler sees a leader style as one that fulfills either the task or the maintenance function within a group.

First let us consider the variables that interact: leader-member relations, task structure, and position power. *Leader-member relations* involve the interpersonal relations the leader has with members of the group. What kind of working relationship exists? Is there mutual trust? Will followers be loyal to the leader? Do the leader and the members like working with each other?

Fiedler discusses *task structure* in terms of four dimensions: (1) goal clarity (how sharply the goal is defined), (2) goal-path multiplicity (the extent to which there are other ways to accomplish the task), (3) decision verifiability (the extent to which accomplishments can be evaluated by objective, logical, or feedback means), and (4) decision specificity (whether the task has only one correct outcome versus several equally good outcomes). The more clear, the more easily verifiable, the more specific, and the fewer paths of accomplishment, the more favorable the task structure is to the leader.

Position power may be analyzed along the lines of social power we considered at the beginning of the chapter. The leader can be judged to be in a low-power or a high-power position. The higher the power position, the more favorable the situation is to the leader. Through these three dimensions, then, we can determine the favorableness of the leader situation.

This leads us to the second benefit of Fiedler's work—help in determining when a given style is most appropriate. Fiedler's approach states that whether a task-oriented leader or a maintenance-oriented leader will be more effective is contingent on the interaction among leader-member relations, task structure, and position power.

An interesting aspect of Fiedler's work is how "task" and "maintenance" orientations are defined. Fiedler determines whether a person is task oriented or maintenance oriented through a written test that asks individuals to define their least-preferred coworker (LPC). On his test, a low LPC score represents a tendency to be task oriented and a high LPC score represents a tendency to be maintenance oriented. Although there is some question as to how this measure predicts whether a person is task oriented or maintenance oriented or why he or she will be successful, research on Fiedler's model has established some positive correlations between LPC scores and success in various situations.

The sense of Fiedler's work is that a person's style is predetermined and somewhat inflexible, so instead of a leader changing styles for different situations, Fiedler suggests changing leaders.

Now let us see how Fiedler puts these variables together. Table 10-1

Table 10-1. Summary of Fiedler's Contingency Model

Situation	Leader-member relations	Task structure	Position power	Appropriate leader style	Favorableness of situation to leader
1	Good	High	Strong	Task	Favorable
2	Good	High	Weak	Task	Favorable
3	Good	Low	Strong	Task	Favorable
4	Good	Low	Weak	Maintenance	Less favorable
5	Fair to poor	High	Strong	Maintenance	Less favorable
6	Fair to poor	High	Weak	Maintenance	Less favorable
7	Fair to poor	Low	Strong	Maintenance	Less favorable
8	Fair to poor	Low	Weak	Task	Unfavorable

Adapted from Fred E. Fiedler, *A Theory of Leadership Effectiveness* (New York: McGraw-Hill, 1967), p. 34. By permission.

summarizes his framework. Situations 1 through 3 represent relatively favorable conditions in which a task orientation is likely to be quite effective. Notice that 1 through 3 represent good leader-member relations. The task is structured in two of the three, and in the remaining unstructured task, the leader is in a high-power position.

In situations 4 through 7, three of the situations have leader-member relations that are relatively poor. In the remaining situation in which leader-member relations are good (situation 4), the task is unstructured and leader position power is weak. In the situations that are relatively unfavorable to the leader, a maintenance-style leader will have greater opportunity for success. Yet, in situation 8, the least favorable, a task leader is likely to have the greatest success even though everything points toward failure. It seems that in this case everything is so bad that only a task-style leader could possibly achieve success.

I've already pointed out that the model does not take into account the potential for a leader to be both task oriented and maintenance oriented. Regardless of your basic orientation, you can learn to adapt to either approach. You can then use the Fiedler model to help determine when you should approach a situation from a strong task orientation and when you should adopt a strong maintenance orientation.

Summary

Leadership is exerting influence to accomplish a specific goal. Effective leadership grows from, or is based on, some real or perceived social power base. Social power—the potential for changing attitudes, beliefs, and behaviors of others—has five bases: coercive power, the potential to punish; reward power, the potential to bestow benefits; legitimate power, resulting from election, selection, or position; expert power, based on superior knowledge; and referent power, based on identification.

Trait theories of leadership have been given renewed emphasis in the last few years. Leaders show greater degrees of ability, sociability, motivation, and communication effectiveness than other members of the group.

Leadership style is also relevant to effectiveness. Some leaders adopt the laissez-faire style of nonleadership; some leaders try to dictate what, when, and how something will be done; and some leaders try to adopt the democratic style of giving the group direction while letting group members participate in decision making. In general, the democratic style yields greatest benefits for the group.

Group variables are not independent. As Fiedler's work has shown, how a leader performs is contingent on the interaction of task structure, leader-member relations, and position power. Fiedler's definition of style indicates either a task approach or a maintenance approach to leadership. Fiedler attempts to determine those circumstances under which a task leader is likely to be most effective and those circumstances under which a maintenance leader is likely to be most effective. From Fiedler we can get a better understanding of the interacting variables and guidance for our attempts to adopt a task or a maintenance approach to our leadership behavior.

11

LEADERSHIP RESPONSIBILITIES

In Chapter 10 I defined leadership and looked at its various components. In this chapter I want to focus on individual responsibilities in exercising leadership in decision-making groups. I will start with suggestions for leadership preparation. I will then present a step-by-step summary of leadership behaviors from the beginning to the end of a group's meeting.

Preparing to Lead

Most of us consider it normal for a person to be appointed or elected to act as leader. We are sometimes not aware that, regardless of whether there is a designated leader, a "real leader" emerges from the group. The appointed leader may prove to be the real leader. Sometimes the appointed leader and one or more others share leadership, and sometimes early in the group's existence or after a long series of tests of leadership, one person emerges as the real leader of the group. So, whether you are the appointed leader or a member of the group, you have the opportunity to share leadership or be the real leader.

Whether you are the nominal leader (the leader in name) or whether you plan to emerge as the real leader, you must work to earn your group's support. You must prepare yourself to lead. Here are some guidelines for this preparation:

1. *As a potential leader, you must have knowledge related to the particular group tasks.* Context determines the emergence and success of the leader far more than possession of any leadership traits. You must grasp enough of the content of the task to recognize which members are contributing effectively and which are not.

2. *To get this knowledge, you must work harder than anyone else in the group.* Leadership is often a question of setting an example. When a group sees a person who is willing to do more than his or her fair share for the good of the group, they are likely to support that person. Of course, such effort often takes a lot of personal sacrifice, but the person seeking to lead must be willing to pay the price.

3. *You must be personally committed to the group goals and needs.* It is quite possible that in any given group for any given situation there may be several who can perform as leaders. To gain and maintain leadership, you need greater enthusiasm for the particular job. When you lose commitment, your leadership may wane and may be transferred to others whose enthusiasm is more tuned to a new set of conditions.

4. *You must be willing to be decisive at key moments in the discussion.* When a leader is unsure of himself or herself, the group may ramble aimlessly. When the leader is unskilled at making decisions, the group can become frustrated and short tempered. When decisions are not made by the designated leader, one or more other persons must assume leadership. Sometimes a leader must make decisions that will be resented; sometimes he, or she must decide between two competing ideas about a course of action, and any decision he or she makes may cause conflict. Nevertheless, a person who is not willing and able to be decisive is not going to maintain leadership for long.

5. *You must interact freely.* No one will opt for a leader who remains silent most of the time. Now this does not mean that you should always dominate the discussion—but no one can know how you think, how you feel, or what insights you have unless you are willing to share your ideas in discussion. Too often people sit back silently, thinking: "If only they would call on me for leadership, I would do a real job." Groups do not want unknown quantities. Perhaps by talking you run the risk of showing your lack of qualifications for leadership, but it is better to find out during early stages of group work whether you can talk sensibly and influence others before you try to function as the leader.

6. *You must develop skill in maintenance functions as well as skill in task functions.* A leader must make others in the group feel good, he or she must be able to contribute a group cohesiveness, and he or she must be able to give credit where it is due. Although a group often has both a task leader and a maintenance leader, the overall leader is equally if not more likely than others to be the one who shows maintenance skills.

So, if you want to be a leader, these are some of the behaviors you must exhibit. However, becoming a leader and carrying out leadership are two different things. Many people reach the top of the leadership pole only to slide slowly to oblivion. Perhaps the key question you must ask yourself when it becomes obvious that you are the leader is, "How am I going to procede with my leadership?"

Leading the Group

The material in this chapter can be considered a checklist for procedure. It is put together as a step-by-step procedure to refer to when you are leading a decision-making group meeting.

Preparing the Meeting Place

Your first job is to set up a comfortable physical setting that will encourage interaction. I discussed the importance of physical environment to group discussion in Chapter 3. Let us briefly review the requirements here. Consider the heat, the light, and the seating. Make sure the room is a comfortable temperature. Make sure that there is enough light. Perhaps most important of all, arrange the seating in a circle or as close to it as possible. People need to be able to see each other to talk freely; moreover, you want to reduce the possibility that the group will perceive the seating arrangement to be by status.

Planning the Agenda

It is your responsibility to plan an agenda for the meeting. When possible, the agenda should be in the hands of the group several days before the meeting. A group needs the opportunity to think about the task before the meeting takes place. How much preparation your group members will make may be based on many factors, but unless the group has an agenda beforehand, members will not have an opportunity for preparation. Moreover, when a group has little idea of what is supposed to happen during the meeting, morale suffers and commitment wanes. Too often when no agenda is planned, the group meeting is a haphazard affair, often frustrating and usually unsatisfying.

The agenda will, of course, be adapted to the group goal and will usually be one of three kinds: (1) a total analysis for a group that is expected to arrive at a decision in one meeting, (2) a partial analysis for one meeting of an ongoing group, or (3) a formal agenda for a general group meeting. Let us consider each.

If a group is expected to arrive at a decision in one meeting, you will want to prepare a total analysis patterned after those suggested on pp. 58–64. Suppose, for instance, that the parent group voted to refer the question "Should yearly dues be raised to $550?" to a committee that you chair. At least a few days before the meeting you should circulate an agenda similar to the following one to all committee members:

Question: Should yearly dues be raised to $550? During the discussion you
should be prepared to consider the following subquestions:

1. Is the group in need of additional funds?

       a.   What areas or programs are suffering?

       b.   Are there additional needs that cannot be met?

2. Can funds be obtained in any other ways?

       a.   Are there areas in which money can be saved?

       b.   Can we get money from external sources?

3. Will a raise to $550 enable the group to meet its needs?

4. Will such a raise have an adverse effect on membership?

       a.   Can present members afford it?

       b.   Will it affect obtaining new members?

During discussion other questions will undoubtedly be considered, but if the group can provide good answers to these questions, it will have a firm basis for resolution of the topic question.

For an ongoing group, the agenda indicates the business that will be handled at that particular meeting. Suppose that this week is the fifth meeting of the long-range planning committee:

Goal: What should be the requirements for the college of liberal arts?

Today's business: Discussion of the Miller Report of a student questionnaire.

       How good was the sample?

       How accurate are the results?

       What effect if any should student views have on the issue?

       What should be the next step?

If the group is an ongoing group that meets regularly to conduct the business of the organization, the agenda is more formal, as in the following established procedure:

       Calling meeting to order

       Reading of the minutes

       Officers' reports

       Committee reports
          Social
          Curriculum
          Library

       Old business
          None

New business

    Jones' proposal to limit expenditures on travel

    Hanley's proposal to conduct quarterly personnel evaluations

    Other

Adjournment

Introducing the Topic and Establishing Procedures

A third responsibility, and one that is especially important for a group's first meeting, is to introduce the topic and establish procedures. At the beginning of a group's existence, commitment may be low for some members, expectations may be minimal, and the general attitude may be questioning. The position of individuals may likely be "We know that many group sessions are a waste of time, and we will take a wait-and-see attitude." A good leader will start the group by drawing a verbal contract and motivating members to live up to it. The leader will answer questions such as: "Why are we here?" "Who got us together?" "What is our mission?" "How much has already been done?" "When are we supposed to finish?" "To whom are we responsible?" "What kinds of responsibilities will each group member have?" "What rules or guidelines for behavior will the group follow?" and "How much will each member be expected to do?" Some of these questions will already have been discussed with individuals, but the first meeting gives the leader a chance to put everything together.

Fulfilling the Gatekeeping Function

The leader is primarily responsible for gatekeeping; however, each group member should operate on the principle of shared leadership responsibilities. It is in this area that leadership skill is most tested. Let us carefully examine several of the most important elements of this responsibility.

We have already discussed the meaning of the gatekeeper role—he or she keeps channels of communication open. The leader should be particularly sensitive to the balance and direction of communication. Yet the leader is often responsible for creating undesirable patterns. Consider the three patterns of group discussion in Figure 11-1, in which lines represent the flow of discussion among the eight participants. Figure 11-1(a) represents a leader-dominated group. The lack of interaction often leads to a rigid, formal, and usually poor discussion. Figure 11-1 (b) represents a more spontaneous group. However, because three people dominate and a few are not heard, conclusions will not represent group thinking. Still, this pattern is by far the most common in work groups. Left to their own devices, some people will speak out more

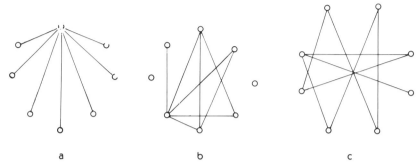

Figure 11-1. Patterns of group discussion.

frequently and some will not speak at all. Figure 11-1(c) represents something closer to the ideal pattern. It illustrates a great deal of spontaneity, a total group representation, and theoretically, the greatest possibility for reliable conclusions.

If the leader takes too active a role in the discussion, a situation such as the one represented in Figure 11-1(a) is likely to occur. Especially during the first few minutes of discussion it is important for leaders to restrain themselves. After the first person has talked, another person should pick up the thread of the discussion. If there is a lull, sit and wait until someone else talks. If you intervene at this point, group members will look for you to talk after each contribution; moreover, members will direct their comments to you instead of to the group.

Your gatekeeping skills will be used most to help a person who is trying to talk and to slow down those who are overly enthusiastic. Although only one person at a time should talk, there are going to be overlaps. Often the person who talks the loudest will get the floor. You don't want to inhibit free flow. But less assertive members of the group can become casualties. When you see that a person is having difficulty getting into the discussion, intercede in the person's behalf with a comment such as, ''Just a second, Mary's been trying to get a point in on this issue—go ahead Mary.''

You will also notice that one or two members will get so involved that they will dominate the discussion. A reminder will usually increase their sensitivity to the need for others to contribute. A comment like, ''Nancy and Jack have given us a really good start on this point—let's hear what others have found that is relevant to this issue.''

Keep in mind that a *group* decision requires *group* participation. It may be that most others are content to let a few carry the load, but it is up to you to see to it that everyone has a part in shaping the decision.

Keeping the Group Thinking

Not only must the leader see to it that the key ideas are discussed, but he or she needs to get maximum value out of each point that is made. The skill that best helps keep the group thinking is the question.

Good use of questioning involves knowing when to ask questions and what kinds of questions to ask. By and large, the leader should refrain from questions that can be answered with yes or no. To ask a group member whether he is satisfied with a point that was just made will not lead very far. After he answers yes or no, you must either ask another question to bring him out or you must change the subject. The two most effective types of questions are those that call for supporting information or open-ended questions that give the member complete freedom of response. For instance, rather than asking John whether he has had any professors that were particularly good lecturers, you could ask, ''John, what are some of the characteristics that made your favorite lecturers particularly effective?'' or ''John, from your experience in listening to speakers, which elements would you select as the most important ones in speaker effectiveness?''

When to ask questions is particularly important. Although we could list fifteen or twenty circumstances, let us focus on four purposes of questioning:

1. *To focus the discussion.* Individual statements usually have a point. The statements relate to a larger point being made, and the general discussion relates to an issue or to an agenda item. You can use questions to determine a speaker's point or to determine the relationship of the point to the issue or agenda item:

> ''Are you saying that the instances of marijuana leading to hard-drug use don't indicate a direct causal relationship?''

> ''How does that information relate to the point that Mary just made?''

> ''In what way does this information relate to whether or not marijuana is a problem?''

2. *To probe for information.* Many statements need to be developed, supported, or dealt with in some way. Yet members of a group often ignore or accept a point without probing it. When the point seems important, the leader should do something with it. For example:

> To verify a source: ''Where did you get that information, Jack?''

> To develop a point: ''That seems pretty important, what do we have that corroborates the point?''

To test the strength of a point: "Does that statement represent the thinking of the group?"

To generate discussion: "That point sounds rather controversial—why should we accept the point as stated?"

3. *To initiate discussion.* During a discussion, there are times when lines of development are apparently ignored or when the group seems ready to agree before sufficient testing has taken place. At these times, it is up to the leader to suggest a starting point for further discussion. For example: "OK, we seem to have a pretty good grasp of the nature of the problem, but we haven't looked at any causes yet. What are some of the causes?"

4. *To deal with interpersonal problems that develop.* Sometimes there is a need to ventilate personal feelings. For example: "Ted, I've heard you make some strong statements on this point. Would you care to share them with us?" At times, the group attacks a person instead of the information that is being presented. An effective response might be: "I know Charley presented the point, but let's look at the merits of the information presented. Do we have any information that counters this point?"

Questions, by themselves, will not make a discussion. In fact, some questions can hurt the discussion that is taking place. The effective leader uses questions sparingly, but decisively.

Coping with Negative Roles

Equally as important as exhibiting and encouraging use of the various task and maintenance roles is dealing with disruptive behaviors exhibited by overly energetic, excessively passive, or knowingly or unknowingly obstreperous members. Let's consider some common disruptive behaviors that must be dealt with.

The Aggressor   The aggressor is the person who works for his own status by criticizing or blaming others when things get rough. His main purpose seems to be to deflate the ego or status of others. One way of dealing with the aggressor is to confront him. Ask him whether he is aware of what he is doing and what effect his behavior is having on the group.

The Blocker   The blocker, related to the aggressor, is a person who goes off on tangents, argues without giving up, or rejects ideas on a personal basis in order to block ideas from gaining group acceptance. The blocker usually has a vested interest in the status quo or a personal reason for opposing the suggested plan. A leader must be concerned with the blocking strategy and should seek group backing for a point before the blocker can establish his or her position. If everyone or nearly everyone favors a point, the leader can present a united front and gain consensus.

The Competer   The competer, similar to the aggressor, is the person who always feels a need to compete with another person or idea, mostly to get attention. His or her ideas are not as important as getting an audience. For instance, if Jane seems to be presenting ideas that the group favors, the competer will bring up another point of view whenever Jane talks so that the group will see him as a thinking person. He competes solely for the joy of the competition. The leader should solicit comments from others and prevent the competer from dominating the discussion.

The Special Pleader   The special pleader has one or two pet ideas. Regardless of the kind of group or its real purpose, the special pleader works on his or her "thing." This person is especially difficult in a new group that is not aware of his or her tactics. An ongoing group soon learns what the person's "thing" is and finds ways around it without hurting his or her feelings.

The Joker   The tension reliever plays a positive role, but the joker is negative. His or her behavior is characterized by clowning, mimicking, or generally disrupting by making a joke of everything. Such people are usually trying to call attention to themselves. They must be the center of attention. A little joking goes a long way. The group needs to get the joker to consider the problem seriously or he or she will be an irritant to other members. One way to proceed is to encourage the joker when tensions need to be released but to ignore him or her when there is serious work to be done.

The Withdrawer   The withdrawer refuses to be a part of the group. This person is a mental dropout. Sometimes he or she is withdrawing from something that was said; sometimes he or she is only showing indifference. Try to draw the person out with questions. Find out what he or she is especially good at so that the group can rely on his or her skills when they are required. Sometimes complimenting the person will being him or her out.

The Monopolizer   The monopolizer needs to talk all the time. Usually, this person is trying to impress the group with the idea that he or she is well read, knowledgeable, and valuable to the group. Such people should, of course, be encouraged when their comments are helpful. But when they are talking too much or when their comments are not helpful, the leader needs to interrupt them and draw others into the discussion.

Summarizing Frequently

Earlier we discussed the important role of the recorder. During a discussion you may play that role or you may delegate it. But to help achieve a good group record of process, you, as leader, must summarize frequently. The decision-making process will involve achieving consensus on many subquestions. These intermediate conclusions are represented by summary statements. For instance, on the topic question "What should be done to lower the crime rate in the United States?" the group would have to reach consensus on each of the following questions:

> What is the problem?
>
> What are the symptoms of the problem? (Draw intermediate conclusions. Ask whether the group agrees.)
>
> What are the causes? (Draw intermediate conclusions on each cause separately or after all causes have been considered. Ask whether the group agrees.)
>
> What criteria should be used to test the solutions?
>
> What is one criterion? (Draw conclusions about each criterion.)
>
> What are some of the possible conclusions? (Determine whether all possible solutions have been brought up.)
>
> What is the best solution?
>
> How does each of the solutions meet the criteria? (Discuss each and draw conclusions about each. Ask whether the group agrees.)
>
> Which solution best meets the criteria? (The conclusion to this final question concludes the discussion. Ask whether all agree.)

During the discussion the group might draw six, eight, ten, or even fifteen conclusions before it is able to arrive at the answer to the topic question. The point is that the group should not arrive at the final conclusion until each of the subordinate questions is answered to the satisfaction of the entire group.

It is up to the leader to emphasize conclusions by summarizing what has been said and seeking consensus on a conclusion. Everyone in the group should realize when the group has arrived at a decision. If left to its own devices, a group will discuss a point for a while, then move on to another before drawing a conclusion. The leader must sense when enough has been said to reach a consensus. Then he or she must phrase the conclusion, subject it to testing, and move on to another area. You should become familiar with phrases that can be used during the discussion:

I think most of us are stating the same points. Are we really in agreement that . . . (state conclusion).

We've been discussing this for a while and I think I sense an agreement. Let me state it, and then we'll see whether it summarizes group feeling. (State conclusion.)

Now we're getting on to another area. Let's make sure that we agree on the point we've just finished. (State conclusion.)

Are we ready to summarize our feelings on this point? (State conclusion.)

Maintaining Necessary Control

Regardless of personal style, as leader, you must maintain control. Remember, absence of leadership leads to chaos. Group members need to feel that someone is in charge. If the group has formal rules, be sure that the rules are followed (bending the rules is necessary, at times, but breaking the rules does not help the group). As leader, remember that some members will be playing negative roles in the discussion; don't let them spoil the outcome. You are in charge, you are responsible, and you have authority. You will need to exercise it on occasion for the benefit of the group. If Johnny is talking for the fortieth time, it is up to you to harness him; if Jack and Mary are constantly sparring with each other, it is up to you to harmonize their differences; if something internal or external threatens the work of the group, it is up to you to deal with it.

Closing the Discussion Effectively

It is up to the leader to determine when the group has finished. A one-meeting group cannot finish until it has completed its task. But as soon as the meeting is finished, you should bring it to a formal close. Ongoing groups need to adjourn when useful discussion seems to have ended for the day, when the day's task is over, or when fatigue is too great. Unfortunately, some groups meet by time instead of by task. Just because you are scheduled to meet from 1:00 to 2:00 P.M. does not mean that you cannot stop at 1:40 if you have finished. And, of course, with an ongoing group you should not let the meeting end until you have set the time and place for the next meeting. You must also see to it that whoever is keeping the group record makes copies of the group's progress and conclusions and distributes them to group members.

Summary

Leadership responsibilities involve preparing yourself to lead and leading the group. Preparing yourself to lead involves working hard to get information related to the topic question, committing yourself to group goals, being willing to be decisive, preparing to interact freely, and sharpening maintenance skills as well as task skills.

Leading the group involves preparing the meeting place, planning an agenda, introducing the topic, fulfilling the gatekeeping function, keeping the group thinking by asking questions, coping with negative roles, summarizing frequently, maintaining necessary control, and bringing the meeting to a close.

Readings for Part Three

Cartwright, Dorwin, and Zander, Alvin (eds.). *Group Dynamics: Research and Theory,* 3rd ed. New York: Harper & Row, 1968. This book is basic to any library of group research and contains excellent material on leadership.

Fiedler, Fred E. *A Theory of Leadership Effectiveness.* New York: McGraw-Hill, 1967. Fiedler's theory has provided the base for an enormous amount of research. Although his theory is still controversial, it is well worth knowing.

Hare, A. Paul. *Handbook of Small Group Research,* 2nd ed. New York: Free Press, 1976. This may be the single most complete survey of small-group research available. The extensive bibliography includes every important work on leadership published prior to 1976.

Hunt, James G., and Larson, Lars L. (eds.). *Crosscurrents in Leadership.* Carbondale, Ill.: Southern Illinois University Press, 1979. An excellent collection of readings that outlines the status of leadership research and clarifies what we can document about leadership.

Shaw, Marvin E. *Group Dynamics: The Psychology of Small Group Behavior,* 3rd ed. New York: McGraw-Hill, 1981. An excellent section summarizing group research.

FOUR

ANALYZING GROUP EFFECTIVENESS

Your responsibility to your group is as both a participant and a critic.
In this one-chapter unit, we will look at the criteria for
evaluating group effectiveness.

12

EVALUATING GROUP DECISION MAKING

Your improvement in group decision making will result, in part, from how well you take advantage of critical appraisal of your work. Not only does feedback help you see your strengths and weaknesses, it may prevent you from falling into bad habits. Some people think that practice alone makes perfect. The fact is that practice of bad habits will only result in more firmly ingrained bad habits! In this chapter we want to look at who has responsibility for feedback, what skills the observer-critic must have, and the focus of criticism, including some of the many forms it can take.

The Critic

At times you may be your own critic. By learning to listen carefully to your own participation and by making mental notes of what you did or did not do, you may provide yourself with useful evaluation. You may also have the opportunity to make audio or video recordings of your participation. Recordings enable you to see or hear your participation, and you can act as a kind of impartial observer in determining where and how you or your group performed.

Of course, the professor has responsibility for criticism. And some of the most valuable criticism will come from that professor.

But for pragmatic as well as educational reasons, a great deal of the criticism you receive will come from your peers. The pragmatic reason concerns classroom size because there may be several decision-making groups working at the same time in class. The professor cannot listen to all of them at the same time, so students will need to help take part of the burden of criticizing. But the educational reason is even better. The student is often motivated to learn more about the decision-making process by functioning as a critic than as a participant. It is likely that as a member of a decision-making groups' class you will have opportunities to function both as a participant and as a critic.

Critical Procedure

As a critic you are likely to find yourself playing three roles: observer, facilitator, and evaluator. Let us look at each of these roles.

Observer

As an observer your goal is to make careful notes of what you see happening. Being an observer gives you a different perspective. Through this perspective you are likely to gain a different insight from that of a participant. As a participant you are likely to concentrate on the decision-making task. It is difficult for the beginner to remember, no less put into practice, the various skills that the decision maker should be using.

As an observer, however, you are freed of the responsibility of thinking about information, and you can spend all of your time focusing on process. Still, skillful observing does not come without practice and without a clear procedure in mind.

First, you must be able to recognize what is taking place. This means you must know the basic skills. Second, you must have a procedure that will work for you. In your first efforts as an observer, you should limit the scope of your observation. Instead of thinking, "I'm going to note everything that happens," you should determine beforehand a list of only a few things to look for. You might start by trying to keep track only of who is talking and to whom. You may also label each of the contributions "task" or "maintenance." It might be wise to focus your attention on one participant at a time, in which case you can look for particular tendencies. You may discover that one person has a tendency to talk too frequently and to seldom make maintenance-type contributions. By considering the behavior of others, you may be able to affect your own group behavior.

Perhaps the most revealing method of analyzing group behavior is to do process analysis. Robert F. Bales has developed a sophisticated method called the Interaction Process Analysis, discussed in his book *Personality and Interpersonal Behavior,*[1] but in this section we want to outline a type of process analysis that is based on guidelines discussed in this textbook. These relatively simple analyses (Figures 12-1 and 12-2) should prove beneficial for you in determining how much each person is participating, in determining the nature of the participation, and in comparing the group's participation with Bales' norms. Bales noted: (1) that 40–60 percent of discussion time is spent on giving and asking for imformation and opinion, (2) that 8–15 percent of discussion time is spent on disagreement, tension, or unfriendliness—behavior that we have discussed as negative roles—and (3) that 16–26 percent of discussion time falls under the headings of agreement, friendliness, or dramatization—behavior that we have discussed as maintenance roles.[2] So, the two norms you can use as guidelines are: (1) approximately half of all

---

[1]Robert F. Bales, *Personality and Interpersonal Behavior* (New York: Holt, Rinehart and Winston, 1971), pp. 99–134.
[2]Bales, p. 96.

Directions: Each time a member of the group speaks, credit the contribution by drawing a line above the circle that represents the person to whom the comment was directed. Do a drawing for each person, and code it with a number in the circle representing that person. The G circle in the center represents comments made to the entire group. An L next to a circle indicates that person is leader. An analysis of this kind enables you to record (1) the number of times each person speaks, (2) the pattern of interaction, and (3) the relationship of leader to the group. The example below is constructed for a six-person group. Draw a circle for each additional person.

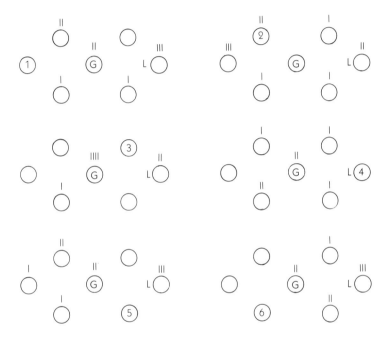

Figure 12-1. Interaction analysis.

discussion time is concerned with information sharing, and (2) group agreement far outweighs group disagreement.

From your comparison, you can see whether your group seems to be acting in a ''normal'' way. If the group is not, the process analysis may lead you to the causes of the difficulty.

EXERCISES

1.

• Observe a group's work. Determine what kind of data you wish to focus on. Prepare an interaction analysis based on Figure 12-2.

Directions: This form is used essentially the same way as Figure 12-1, except that each comment is labeled. You can use letters of the alphabet, numbers, or other symbols to represent any contribution you wish to identify. In the following analysis, the observer is interested in differentiating between task and maintenance statements. 1 represents a task comment, + represents a maintenance comment, and 0 is used for a comment that cannot be identified.

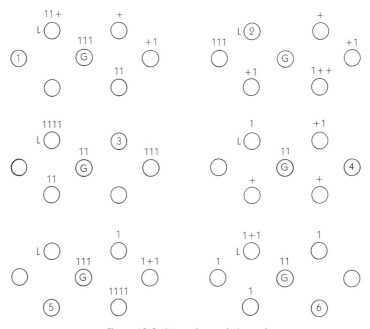

Figure 12-2. Interaction analysis—role.

2. Observe one person's behavior. (a) Prepare an interaction analysis based on Figure 12-2 for that person. (b) Make notes characterizing the use of the particular skills you are observing.

Facilitator

A *facilitator* is a person who helps a group with process during the discussion. By "process" I mean use of various skills other than giving and receiving information or opinions. Because participants are immersed in the information that is being presented, they are likely to lose sight of the need to support, clarify, question, and so forth.

One goal of the facilitator is to prompt members of the group to use a skill when it is needed. Let us use the need for a summary as an example. Some groups go through an entire discussion without ever summarizing what was said or what was decided. As a facilitator, you could prompt the group whenever a summary would be useful. Recall that a summary is essential whenever the group has reached consensus on an issue and before it goes on to something else. When you sense that consensus is reached, you can prompt someone to make a summary at that time. By doing so, you facilitate the group's procedure.

A second important function of the facilitator is to help the group probe information that is being taken for granted. Suppose a group is discussing means of implementing a 10 percent budget cut. George suggests that postage can be cut in half. If no one follows up on the suggestion, you might say "Will a cut in postage affect potential sales?" The group may ignore your question—on the other hand, the question may remind the group that any suggested solution must be tested against potential costs. The question might then trigger further necessary discussion.

The role of facilitator provides excellent pragmatic and educational value. First, a good facilitator helps a group to keep some attention on process—the facilitator reminds the group of when the use of a skill would be appropriate. Moreover, acting as facilitator can be of excellent educational value to the person playing the role. A facilitator must be familiar with key process skills. So, assigning a person to facilitate puts a burden of responsibility on him or her to study the skills. If you serve as a facilitator, you are likely to find that later on in your own group work you will pay attention to process and therefore try to use some of the necessary skills without prompting.

Facilitators can be assigned one to a group or to each person in the group. When there is a facilitator for each person, the facilitator and the participant can form a team. The facilitator can closely monitor his or her partner's participation and make suggestions about when to talk, what kind of comment to make, and so forth.

EXERCISES

Have each person in the group play the role of facilitator for a given period of time during that group's discussion. To sharpen practice, the skills that people use should be clearly identified. For instance, during the first practice round, the facilitator should focus on paraphrasing, questioning, gatekeeping, and summarizing.

Evaluator

The *evaluator* has the responsibility of talking about what the group accomplished and how well they did it. At the end of the discussion the evaluator should give a running summary of what happened. Being an evaluator requires taking careful notes. Sometimes two or three critics are assigned to each group and at the end they form a panel for criticism.

Evaluation may be oral or written. At the end of this chapter we will talk about many of the approaches to evaluation and suggest several forms for your use. As preparation for evaluation you may find the interaction analyses excellent means of note taking.

Presenting Criticism—Feedback

Whether you are playing the role of an observer, a facilitator, or an evaluator, you must understand how to effectively give feedback. Feddback takes three forms: (1) describing behavior, (2) praise, and (3) criticism.

Describing behavior means accurately recounting specific observable behavior without labeling the behavior good or bad, right or wrong. The most difficult part of describing behavior is avoiding the tendency to describe in judgmental terms. For example: Beth tells the group about her experience with the employee review system that is being replaced. In the middle of her narrative, Ann interrupts to tell the group about a similar experience she had. Beth, annoyed, says, "Why are you so rude, Ann?" Such a statement does not *describe* the behavior, it judges it. Beth would be describing Ann's behavior if she said, "Ann, were you aware that you started telling your experience before I had a chance to finish telling mine?"

As a method of personal feedback within the group setting, judgmental comments have two weaknesses. First, judgment does not inform. When Beth says, "Why are you so rude?" she is not providing the basis for the judgment. Ann may not know what she has done to bring about Beth's reaction. Second, judgment is likely to trigger a counter-judgment that will change the subject and further weaken the positive communication climate that is necessary in group work. When Beth says, "Why are you so rude?" Ann is likely to feel attacked. To protect herself, Ann may lash out at Beth with "Who do you think you are calling me rude? I'm not the one who is always sounding so superior!" Suddenly Ann and Beth are arguing about something that is totally unrelated to the issue.

On the other hand, if Beth were to say, "Ann, were you aware that you started telling your experience before I had a chance to finish mine?" Ann might reply, "Well, I wouldn't have to interrupt if you weren't so long-winded." And the conflict might still occur. But because Beth's statement is a description, Ann is not likely to take it as a judgment.

Following are three more examples of personal feedback that describe behavior:

Jack: Bill, you smile when your other behavior seems to be saying that you are angry.
Wendy: Jed, when you criticize, your voice has a very sharp tone.
Andy: Mark, whenever Alice joins the group you are all smiles.

Nonevaluative description is probably the best form for personal feedback.

Praise is a positive reaction to what a person has said or done. Everyone needs to feel successful at something. When you observe that a person has done something quite well or when you hear a person say something in a particularly good way, you should feel free to tell that person about it. For example:

Sally: Gwenn, that comment was right on target. You're very perceptive.
Jim: Gail, I really like the way you outlined the problem. You make the whole thing so clear to me.
Drew: Guy, that was nice of you to share your lunch with Pete. You're a very warm-hearted person.

Not only does praise fulfill the supporter role, but it gives direct feedback.

Criticism is judgment of behavior, and more often than not, it's negative judgment. Criticism should be avoided if possible. If a person asks for criticism, you should proceed by first describing behavior and then judging it. For instance:

Agnes: How do you like my idea?
Joyce: You stated it clearly, but you didn't give any support. I really can't support it if I don't know whether it will work.

Dean: What do you think of my report?
Rick: There were a great number of typographical errors and several mistakes in grammar. I thought your report was hurried because it contained many mistakes.

Whenever you are in a situation where you need to give feedback, the following guidelines should prove helpful.[3]

1. *Make sure that giving feedback is appropriate in the interpersonal context.* It is safest to withhold feedback until it is asked for. Feedback becomes dysfunctional if a person is not interested in hearing it. Even the people who seem willing to listen to any kind of comments may not always be receptive to what you want to say.

If a person has not asked for feedback, but you feel that some feedback would benefit him or her, you should be careful about your timing. Look for

---

[3]Several of these suggestions were first articulated in the *1968 Summer Reading Book* of the National Training Laboratories Institute of Applied Behavioral Sciences.

signs of receptiveness and watch verbal or nonverbal cues indicating that some feedback would be welcomed. If you are not sure, ask. You might say, for example, "Would you like to hear my comments about the way you handled the meeting?" Remember, however, that even if the person says yes, you must proceed carefully.

2. *Preface a negative statement with a positive one whenever possible.* Feedback need not be negative, although for some reason most people think that it is (as if all they hear about are things that are wrong). When you are planning to criticize, it is a good idea to start with praise. But use a little common sense. Do not start with superficial praise and then follow it with crushing criticism, such as: "Betty, that's a pretty blouse you have on, but you did a perfectly miserable job of running the meeting." A better approach would be: "Betty, you did a good job of drawing Sam into the discussion. He usually sits through an entire meeting without saying a word. But you seem hesitant to use the same power to keep the meeting on track. You seem content to let anybody talk about anything, even if it is unrelated to the agenda." The praise here is significant. If you cannot give significant praise, then don't try. Empty comments made just to be "nice" are worthless.

3. *Be as specific as possible.* In the situation just discussed, it would not have been helpful to say, "You had some leadership problems." If the person wasn't in control, say so. If the person failed to get agreement on one item before moving on to another, say so. The more specific the feedback, the more effectively the person will be able to deal with the information.

4. *Feedback should concern recent behavior.* No one is helped much by hearing about something he or she did last week or last month. Feedback is best when it is fresh. If you have to spend time re-creating a situation and refreshing someone's memory, the feedback will probably be ineffective.

5. *Criticism should be directed at behavior that can be changed.* It is pointless to remind people of shortcomings over which they have no control. It may be true that Jack would be a better leader if he had a deeper voice, but telling him so will not improve his leadership skill. Telling him he needs to work on stating summaries or getting agreement on issues is helpful because he can change these behaviors.

6. *Show the person you are criticizing what they can do to improve.* Do not limit your comments to what a person has done wrong. Tell the person how what was done could have been done better. If Gail, the chairperson of a committee, cannot get her members to agree on anything, you might suggest that she try phrasing her remarks to the committee differently. For

example: "Gail, when you think discussion is ended, say something like 'It sounds as if we agree that our donation should be made to a single agency. Is that correct?' "

Evaluation

Now that we have considered the bases for criticism, we can consider additional instruments for analyzing group decisions, individual participation, and leadership.

Evaluating the Method of Reaching a Decision

Figure 12-3 gives us an opportunity to look at the group decision. The theory behind this instrument is that since the group's goal is to arrive at a decision, a decision-based critical instrument will consider the end product of group communication. As you will see, this instrument calls for you to discuss two major questions:

1. *Did the group arrive at a decision?* Just because a group meets for discussion does not necessarily mean that it will arrive at a decision. As foolish as it may seem, there are some groups that thrash away for hours only to adjourn without having arrived at a decision. Of course, some groups discuss such serious problems that a decision cannot be reached without several meetings, but I am not talking about a group that plans to meet later to consider the issue further—I mean the group that "finishes" without arriving at a decision. Failure to arrive at a decision results in total frustration and disillusionment.

2. *Was the group decision a good one?* Earlier I defined a good decision as one that results from logical procedure and that results in group

---

Was the group goal clearly articulated as a question of fact, evaluation, or policy? Explain.

Did the group consider the key issues appropriate to resolution of that type of question? Explain.

Was quality information presented to serve as a base or foundation for the decision? Explain.

Were the data fully discussed? Explain.

Is the decision defensible? Explain.

Is the decision likely to work? Explain.

Figure 12-3. Decision analysis. Did the group arrive at a decision? Explain. Was the decision a good one? Consider the questions above.

satisfaction. To give you the chance to examine the decision in the most comprehensive manner possible, I suggest applying the following criteria:

a.   Was the group goal clearly articulated as a question of fact, evaluation, or policy?

b.   Did the group consider the key issues appropriate to resolution of that type of question?

c.   Was quality information presented to serve as a base or foundation for the decision?

d.   Were the data fully discussed?

e.   Is the decision defensible? In addition to considering the key issues, this criterion asks whether the group has prepared a written record that can be transmitted along with the decision to the parent group.

f.   Is the decision likely to work? Although there is no way of telling beforehand, the substance of the group written record may give a clue.

Evaluating Group Members

A group will have difficulty functioning without members who are willing and able to meet the task and maintenance functions of the group. The next instrument (Figure 12-4) incorporates many of the skills considered earlier in this text and provides a relatively easy-to-use checklist that can be kept for each individual.

Preparation
    Has good information
    Understands the issues
Presentation
    Gives information
    Expedites
    Analyzes
    Clarifies
    Relieves tension
    Harmonizes
    Gatekeeps
    Supports
Negative roles
    Monopolizes
    Withdraws
    Is aggressive
    Is a jokester

Write an analysis of the person's group participation based on this checklist.

Figure 12-4. Member analysis. Rate each participant on this list.

Evaluating Leadership

Although some group discussions are leaderless, no discussion should be leadershipless. An important element of the evaluation process is to consider the nature of the leadership. If there is an appointed leader, and most groups have one, you can focus on that individual. If the group is truly leaderless, you must consider all attempts at leadership by the various members or determine who emerges as the real leader. The leadership analysis checklist (Figure 12-5) provides an easy-to-use instrument for evaluating group leadership.

EXERCISE

Each classroom group should be given or allowed to select a task (a topic question) that requires some research. Give each group approximately 30 to 40 minutes for discussion. While group A is discussing, members of group B should observe. After the discussion group B should give feedback during the remainder of the class period. For practice in using the various instruments, one observer could be asked to do a process analysis (Figure 12-1 or 12-2), another could be asked to do a decision analysis (Figure 12-3), another could be asked to do a member analysis (Figure 12-4), and a fourth could be asked to do a leadership analysis (Figure 12-5). During the next class period, group B should discuss and group A should observe and critique. The kinds of questions that can be used for this assignment are:

What should be done to improve parking (advising; registration) on campus?

What should be done to increase the participation of women in college or university athletic (administrative; teaching) programs?

Preparation to lead
    Works hard
    Understands topic
    Shows commitment
Leading the group
    Has an agenda
    Opens discussion effectively
    Creates and maintains a suitable atmosphere
    Gatekeeps
    Questions
    Summarizes
    Harmonizes
    Maintains control
    Deals with conflict
    Brings the meeting to a satisfactory close

Figure 12-5. Leadership analysis. For each of these descriptions, rate the leadership: 1, high; 2, good; 3, average; 4, fair; 5, poor.

Summary

Part of your improvement in group decision making will result from taking advantage of the critical appraisal you receive from self-analysis, comments from your professor, or information from your peers.

During the course or in meetings you are likely to gain experience as an observer, as a facilitator, and as an evaluator. An observer makes careful notes of what takes place. A facilitator helps a group with process. An evaluator is responsible for showing the group what it has accomplished and how well it was accomplished.

Regardless of the role you play, you must understand how to describe behavior, how to praise, and how to give negative criticism. Under any circumstances, feedback should: be appropriate, contain positive as well as negative statements, be specific, concern recent behavior, be directed toward' something that can be changed, and be accompanied by a method for improvement.

Evaluation instruments can be directed toward the group process, the decision, individual participation, or leadership.

Readings for Part Four

Brilhart, John D. *Effective Group Discussion,* 3rd ed. Dubuque, Iowa: Wm. C. Brown, 1978. See pp. 232–255.

Patton, Bobby R., and Giffin, Kim. *Decision-Making Group Interaction,* 2nd ed. New York: Harper & Row, 1978. See Part 4, pp. 193–239.

Potter, David, and Andersen, Martin P. *Discussion in Small Groups: A Guide to Effective Practice,* 3rd ed. Belmont, Calif.: Wadsworth, 1976. See Chapter 11, pp. 197–211.

APPENDIX: CHECKLISTS

Whether or not your assignments are made by type of question, once you have identified the type of question you will be resolving it may be useful to go through the following checklists before your group finalizes its plans for procedure. These checklists serve as both reviews of information covered within the text and as illustrations of further applications of that information.

I assume that during your group's planning stages, members will be flexible in their view of the topic question. As deliberation begins, you are rarely able to say that the wording you start with is the only wording that is appropriate. Even when you are satisfied with the goal suggested by the person or parent group responsible for forming your decision-making group, it is still wise to take some time to consider variations in wording of the question. The details of the checklists follow.

Checklist for Discussing a Question of Fact

"What is the status of the ABC Company's profit-sharing plan?" "Did the raw material used in the project come from black market sources?" and "Will gold go up significantly by the end of the year?" are examples of questions of fact (classification, descriptive evaluation, and prediction) that you are likely to be discussing in your groups.

Refer to this checklist as your group proceeds with its deliberations. Make sure that the group has arrived at a satisfactory answer to each question.

Following the checklist is a summary discussion of the material relevant to each question.

Question of Fact

1. Is your group goal best accomplished with a topic question that classifies, makes a descriptive judgment, or makes a prediction?

2. Is your goal best met with an open or a closed phrasing of a question of fact?

3. What research strategy should you follow? Comprehensive or divison of labor?

4. What is the appropriate analysis for the question?

5. Is every conclusion clearly stated and well supported?

6. Are you keeping a complete record of each decision?

1. Is your group goal best accomplished with a topic question that classifies, makes a descriptive judgment, or makes a prediction? As we have seen, the question of fact focuses on gathering facts and drawing conclusions. If your group wants to make comparative evaluations or recommendations for change, it should rephrase the question to an appropriate question of evaluation or policy.

If your group is not yet ready to commit itself to a topic question that may require tremendous time expenditure, it may want to phrase a question of fact as a step in determining its ultimate goal. Suppose a task force is brought together to consider the problem of crime on campus. Perhaps a few recent incidents have triggered alarm that has resulted in a cry for the task force. Yet, the task force members are not sure of the need for launching into a long-term investigation of policy recommendations. To test the water, the group may decide to consider the question "Is there an increase in the amount of serious crime on campus this year?" Such wording gives the group a chance to investigate the size of the problem before the group commits itself to the obligation of making recommendations. If the group finds that crime has not really increased over the last several years or that the amount of crime is not really significant, the group can end its deliberations. If, on the other hand, the group finds that crime has increased substantially and that the increase is restricted to instances of aggravated robbery or rape, the group may decide to redefine its goal by restating the question as one of policy, such as "What should the university do to cope with the problem of increases in serious crime on campus?"

2. Is your goal best met with an open or a closed phrasing of a question of fact? As mentioned in Chapter 4, a closed question of fact restricts discussion to a yes or no answer. For example, the question "Is the XYZ corporation in violation of antitrust laws?" is resolved when the group answers yes or no.

An open question of fact, on the other hand, takes a broad look at the subject area. The phrasing "What corporations are currently acting in violation of antitrust laws?" is an open question of fact. It cannot be resolved with a simple yes or no.

The choice between closed or open phrasing is made in part by what the group is trying to accomplish. If the group is called upon to consider only the actions of the XYZ corporation, then the closed question would be most appropriate for consideration. If, however, the group is a fact-finding commission that has the authority to root out violators, choosing an open question is more appropriate.

The advantage of a closed question of fact is that it provides a sharper focus for discussion. The group knows its goal and is unlikely to be drawn off course.

There are, however, two disadvantages to closed wording. The first is the tendency for the group to move directly to consideration of support for the affirmative or negative position without devoting enough time to background. The second is the likelihood that the discussion will evolve into a debate, with some group members taking the affirmative and some the negative. Nevertheless, when the closed-question phrasing better meets the goals of the group, it should be selected regardless of the potential problems.

3. What research strategy should you follow? Individually or collectively, members of the group must determine a research strategy. With some topic questions it may be appropriate for each member to attempt a comprehensive search for material. For instance, for the question "What criteria have been used in the selection of college department heads?" it would seem an appropriate research strategy for each person to find all the information possible. If, on the other hand, the question is "What are the major differences in the proposals offered by the five major companies competing for the City of Cincinnati cable television franchise?" the group might adopt a strategy of division of labor: each member could be assigned to take a comprehensive look at only one or two of the proposals. The group would first decide the criteria for examining each proposal so that each person would be looking at the same considerations. For instance, the group might decide to consider costs, benefits to the community, and flexibility. After initial research is done, the group could share its findings and begin a comparison of the various proposals.

Research strategy depends on such questions as the size or scope of the task, the amount of potential information, the proposed use of the information, and the variety of sources of information.

4. What is the appropriate analysis for the question? Once the group has agreed on the wording of the question, each person has the opportunity, if not the responsibility, to make an independent analysis. Although tradition calls for the suggested procedure to be in the hands of the leader, we have already discussed the advantages of individual members making independent analyses.

When the group begins its actual deliberations, it will determine the structure to be followed. If time is taken to make this decision early in the group's deliberations, considerable time will be saved in the long run.

You should keep in mind, however, that although the group may agree on a procedure, few, if any, groups move linearly through the steps of analysis. Even when a group has agreed on a logically sound procedure, there will be irrelevant comments, efforts to jump forward, digressions, reversals in direction, and so forth. Crowell[1] found that even well-prepared groups are likely to proceed in a spiraling manner.

If, however, no one tries to give the group structure, chaos is likely to reign. Even relatively well-organized deliberation may appear to be messy, but some order is a necessity. Groups that create or adopt a structure for their deliberations are likely to accomplish a task more quickly than groups that proceed with no structure. Moreover, the presence of some structure is likely to lead to higher-quality decisions. While there is no research support to show that any one structure works best under all circumstances, I suggest following the order that is based on solid logical analysis of the question.

Now let us review the stock analyses for questions of fact. You will recall that analysis of any kind of question of fact is based on issues of definition, data, and quality. And in Chapter 5, I outlined the application of this analysis to each of the three major types of questions. But sometimes the entire analysis cannot be

---

[1]Thomas M. Scheidel and Laura Crowell, "Idea Development in Small Discussion Groups," *Quarterly Journal of Speech,* Vol. 50 (1964), pp. 140–145.

made at once—the group must be alerted to these possibilities so that the group members are saved unnecessary work.

Let us illustrate such a situation by analyzing the question "What is the status of the company profit-sharing plan?" We can quickly determine the three broad questions:

a.   What are the definitions of "status" and "profit-sharing plan"?

b.   What are the data relevant to the definitions?

c.   Are there extenuating circumstances that might affect our assessment?

A look at this analysis will show that any problem in discussion is likely to occur with definition. Defining status as a "condition" and profit-sharing plan as a "retirement plan in which a portion of company profits funds employee retirement" will not get the group very far. In this case the group will have to define the facts of the plan in order to determine their status. Because the way this is done will affect what takes place later, the group will not want to go much further in analysis or research until they have agreed on such facts as: (a) total money in the plan, (b) level of contribution, (c) method of receiving funds, and so forth. So, even though the broad analysis can be done quickly, sometimes the total analysis will require group participation, and the resolution of the question will have to be done in stages.

5.   Is every conclusion clearly stated and well supported? Although your question of fact calls for one final decision, that decision is based on several decisions along the way. How good your decision is perceived to be and how much impact that decision will have on others is likely to depend on whether others understand how and why you arrived at your conclusions. Clear statement of each decision will show how you got to that decision and a summary of the data will show why that conclusion was warranted. Recall that conclusions that sound reasonable to the group and that may be arrived at by consensus may still be faulty. Groupthink is an all-too-common problem with decision-making groups. You can protect against groupthink as well as provide substantiation for those who request it by having a summary of the data that led to each conclusion.

6.   Are you keeping a complete record of each decision? This final check goes hand in hand with the last one. Regardless of how well each conclusion is stated and how much data are used to substantiate that conclusion, you cannot demonstrate the logic of your procedure without a written record. Every decision must be accompanied by a complete written statement of that decision.

Checklist for Discussing a Question of Evaluation

"Which department has been most effective in implementing new personnel procedures?" "Was Perkins the most valuable worker in the division last month?" and "Is the Cason method better for achieving increased levels of production than our current method?" represent the kinds of questions of evaluation that are asked in business, education, and social settings.

The checklist for a discussion of a question of evaluation uses essentially the same questions as the checklist for a question of fact.

Refer to this checklist as your group proceeds with its deliberations. Make sure that the group has arrived at a satisfactory answer to each question.

Following the checklist is a summary discussion of the material relevant to each question.

Question of Evaluation

1. Is your goal accomplished with a topic question that makes a direct comparison between two entities or with one that evaluates an entity on the basis of a universal standard?

2. Is your goal best met with an open or a closed phrasing of a question of evaluation?

3. What research strategy should you follow? Comprehensive or division of labor?

4. What is the appropriate analysis for the question?

5. Is every conclusion clearly stated and well supported?

6. Are you keeping a complete record of each decision?

1. Is your goal accomplished with a topic question that makes a direct comparison between two entities or with one that evaluates an entity on the basis of a universal standard? If your group wants only to determine the nature of the facts or if it wants to make recommendations for a change, then you should rephrase the question to be an appropriate question of fact or policy.

As with the selection of a question of fact, your group may select a question of evaluation as an interim question before phrasing a more comprehensive question of policy.

If, for instance, a company is concerned about the effectiveness of its public relations program, it may anticipate a comprehensive analysis of recommendations for improvement. Because such an endeavor would require a long-range commitment of manpower and funds, the company may decide to first compare its program with that of one of its closest competitors. The decision-making group would then ask the question "Is our public relations program as good as XYZ's?" If the group finds that its program is as good, they may then decide there is no need for considering major changes. If, on the other hand, the group finds that the program is not nearly as good as XYZ's, the group might decide to redefine the problem by restating the question as "What should be done to improve the quality of our public relations program?"

2. Is your goal best met by phrasing an open or a closed question of evaluation? Remember, a closed question restricts the outcome to a yes or no answer; an open question allows for the comparison of several options. If the group sees its evaluation in terms of one item or one level of comparison, a closed question is preferable. Two such examples are: "Is our public relations program as good as XYZ's?" and "Is our management training program academically sound?"

On the other hand, the group may be looking for one or more answers from a group of possibilities. In order to determine one or a small number of answers, the open question would be more appropriate. The following examples illustrate such phrasings: "What local company has the best public relations program?" or "Which are the most effective training programs in the corporation?"

3. What research strategy should you follow? Individually or collectively, members of the group must determine a research strategy. The advice for determining such a strategy is essentially the same as that given for a question of fact. Your strategy depends on the size or scope of the task, the amount of potential information, and the variety of sources of information. For a question such as "Is our management training program academically sound?" it is appropriate for each member of the group to make a comprehensive search. For the question "What local company has the best public relations program?" on the other hand, the group might decide to have each person look at companies in a certain locality. Later, the group could share what it has found and begin a comparison of the various companies' programs.

4. What is the appropriate analysis of the question? When the group begins its deliberations, it will determine the structure to be followed. The time taken to make this decision early in the group's deliberations will save time in the long run. But, as I have mentioned, you should expect that during the actual discussion the group may still go in various directions. Even so, everyone in the group should try to keep some structure in the discussion.

Now let us review the stock analysis for questions of evaluation. You will recall that analysis of any kind of question of evaluation is based on issues of criteria, data, and quality. Establishing criteria will probably cause the group the greatest difficulty. Let us illustrate group procedure by analyzing the question "Is our public relations program better than XYZ's?" We can quickly determine four broad issues:

a. What are the criteria for determining a "better public relations program"?

b. What are the facts related to each of the programs?

c. Which set of facts better meets the criteria?

d. Are there extenuating circumstances that might affect our assessment?

A problem will occur in listing criteria and determining relative importance because our opinions are likely to be a product of our own value systems. It is at this point that we must apply the tests of criteria discussed in Chapter 8: (1) whether the criteria have proven to be good measures in the past, (2) whether authority figures accept these criteria, (3) whether the criteria fit the needs of the group, and (4) whether the criteria can be justified by reasons and evidence. Suppose that three of the criteria listed are (a) "Is our program improving the image of our company better than XYZ's?" (b) "Is the community receiving more accurate information about our company than it is receiving about theirs?" and (c) "Does our program have better personnel than theirs?" The first two criteria would probably be regarded as more important than the third, but the first two concern the effects of the programs. How good the personnel are means little if both programs are working well. If the program is not meeting the first two criteria, the third one becomes more important. Once criteria have been listed in order of priority, the rest of the discussion should go relatively well.

5. Is every conclusion clearly stated and well supported? Although your question of evaluation calls for one final decision, that decision is based on several decisions along the way. As with consideration of any other type of question, how good your decision is perceived to be and how much impact that decision will have on others is likely to depend on whether others understand how and why you arrived at your conclusions. You protect against groupthink as well as provide substantiation for those who request it by having a summary of the data that led to each conclusion.

6. Are you keeping a complete record of each decision? Again, you need to remind yourself of the importance of a written record of each conclusion and its support.

Checklist for Discussing a Question of Policy

"Should the corporation begin a management training program?" and "What should the university do to cope with the problem of major crimes in campus dormitories?" are examples of the kinds of policy questions decision-making groups are called on to resolve.

The checklist for a discussion of a question of policy uses essentially the same questions as the ones for a question of fact and a question of evaluation.

Refer to this checklist as your group proceeds with its deliberations. Make sure that the group has arrived at a satisfactory answer to each question.

Following the checklist is a summary discussion of the material relevant to each question.

Question of Policy

1. Is your goal accomplished with a topic question that considers a change in policy?

2. Is your goal best met with an open or a closed phrasing of a question of policy?

3. What research strategy should you follow? Comprehensive or division of labor?

4. What is the appropriate analysis for the question?

5. Is every conclusion clearly stated and well supported?

6. Are you keeping a complete record of each decision?

1. Is your goal accomplished with a topic question that considers a change in policy? If your group wants only to determine the nature of the facts or to make a comparative evaluation, you should rephrase the question to be a question of fact or evaluation. Since the great majority of decision-making groups see

policy making as their primary goal, mastery of the skills of discussing a question of policy is a necessity.

2. Is the goal of the group best met by phrasing an open or a closed question of policy? Remember that a closed question of policy restricts discussion to the evaluation of a single policy, such as "Should auto manufacturers focus the majority of their research and development monies on the electric car?" Ultimately the group will arrive at a yes or a no answer. If the answer is no, the group may or may not feel compelled to suggest alternatives to the policy in question.

An open question of policy looks at a broad subject area and encourages the group to arrive at a solution that should be implemented. The group may ask the question "On what kinds of research and development should auto manufacturers focus the majority of their money at this time?" As with questions of fact and questions of evaluation, the advantages and disadvantages of open and closed phrasings pertain.

3. What research strategy should you follow? The advice for determining a research strategy for a question of policy is much the same as that for developing a strategy of research for any other type of question. It depends on such questions as the size or scope of the task, the amount of potential information, and the variety of sources of information.

To prepare for the question "Should the corporation offer a management training program?" it would be appropriate for each person to find all the information possible. On the other hand, to prepare for the question "How should we structure our sales campaign to compete with the largest companies in the city?" there may be a necessity for division of labor. Each member of the group could research sales campaign planning at one or more of the companies in the city. Then the group could pool its material and draw conclusions from it.

4. What is the appropriate analysis for the question? You will recall that analysis of a question of policy is based on the four issues of problem, cause, cure, and cost. The problem you are likely to encounter with a question of policy is whether or not there is a problem area that needs to be explored. Let us contrast two questions of policy: (1) "What should the university do to control the problem of crime in dormitories?" and (2) "Who should be awarded the outstanding teacher prize for the year?" With the first question, all four issues will need to be explored. You cannot determine what to do about crime until you fully understand the size and scope of the problem and what has caused the problem. In these cases, the nature and causes of the problem will provide the basis for the criteria on which solutions will be measured. With the outstanding teacher award question, there is no problem to be solved. Since there is no problem to serve as a base for development of criteria, criteria will have to be developed separately as they are in questions of evaluation. The analysis for the outstanding teacher question will look something like this:

Question: Who should be awarded the outstanding teacher prize for the year?

       a. What are criteria for determining an outstanding teacher?

       b. Who are the nominees?

       c. Which of the moninees best meets the criteria?

    d.   Are there any negative characteristics that outweigh the ways in which each nominee meets the criteria?

Another type of question of policy that offers similar problems is illustrated by the following question: "Should Martin Luther King Jr.'s birthday be celebrated as a national holiday?" Again, with this question there is no problem as such. But in place of discussing a problem you can consider forces favoring and forces opposing such a move (a force-field analysis). Then the final two issues can be cure/benefits: What are the benefits of making it a national holiday? What are the costs? Are there any disadvantages that outweigh the benefits? In outline form, the analysis would look like this:

Question: Should Martin Luther King Jr.'s birthday be celebrated as a national holiday?

    a.   What are the forces in favor of and opposed to such a plan? (causes, force-field analysis)

    b.   What are the benefits? (cure)

    c.   Are there disadvantages that outweigh the benefits? (cost)

With the discussion of any question of policy, members of the group need to be flexible in determining which issues are most appropriate for that particular question.

    5.   Is every conclusion drawn clearly stated and well supported? With a question of policy, perhaps more than any other type of question, you must be conscious of the need for clear statements of decisions and support. In the first place, the analysis is likely to be more complicated, so there are likely to be more subquestions considered. In the second place, because you are recommending a course of action other people and groups are going to be even more interested in the bases for your recommendations. Remember, you protect against groupthink as well as provide substantiation for those who request it by having a summary of the data that led to each conclusion.

    6.   Are you keeping a complete record of each decision? This final check goes hand in hand with the last one. Regardless of how well each conclusion is stated and how much data were used to substantiate that conclusion, you cannot demonstrate the logic of your procedure without a written record. No decision should be made at any place in the discussion without a complete written statement of that decision.

INDEX